Handbook for Implementing an ISO 14001

Environmental Management System

A Practical Approach

SECOND EDITION

By John Kinsella and
Annette Dennis McCully

COVER PHOTO: Port of Houston
PHOTO CREDIT: GILBREATH COMMUNICATIONS

Published by Shaw Environmental, Inc.
First Edition, 1999
Second Edition, 2003
ISBN: 0-9671475-2-2
Library of Congress Catalog Card Number: 99-62931

Handbook for Implementing an ISO 14001 Environmental Management System: A Practical Approach
By John Kinsella and Annette Dennis McCully.
Betty Hageman, Art Director
Susan Milligan, Editor

Copyright © 2003 by Shaw Environmental, Inc. All rights reserved. No part of this publication may be reproduced, stored in a retrieval system, or transmitted, in any form or by any means, electronic, mechanical, photocopying, recording, or otherwise, without the prior written permission of the publisher: Shaw Environmental, Inc., 19909-120th Avenue NE, Suite 101, Bothell, WA 98011.

Standard quotes extracted with the permission of ASTM, from ANSI/ISO 14001, copyright ISO, ANSI, and ASTM. The complete standard may be obtained from ASTM, 100 Barr Harbor Drive, West Conshohocken, PA 19428, phone: 610-832-9585 fax: 610-832-9555, e-mail: *service@astm.org*, website: *http://www.astm.org*.

Acknowledgments
With Thanks to Contributors: Jim Kliesch, ACEEE; Richard Ellis, Advanced Waste Management Systems; Norman Ingram, BP Exploration Alaska Inc.; Dave Church and Randy Daugherty, BVQI; Mike Cycyota and Ricardo Valverde, Baxter International, Inc.; Chuck Tellas, Milan Screw Products, Inc.; Laura Fiffick, Port of Houston Authority; Alan Ricketts, Trus Joist, a Weyerhaeuser Company; and Paul Steucke, U.S. Army, Ft. Lewis, WA.

 PRINTED IN THE UNITED STATES OF AMERICA WITH SOY INK ON RECYCLED, ACID-FREE PAPER

Contents

Introduction 3

1 Environmental Management Systems 7

2 Companies That Have Benefited from an EMS 15

3 The Evolution of International Management System Standards 23

4 Structure of ISO 14001 35

5 4.2 Environmental Policy 43

6 4.3 Planning 51

7 4.4 Implementation and Operation 65

8 4.5 Checking and Corrective Action 87

9 4.6 Management Review 103

10 The Certification Process 109

11 Some Continual Improvement Insights 121

A Appendix A – Glossary 131

B Appendix B – Resources: Contributors, Standards, and Websites 137

Index 149

An EMS reduces negative impacts on the environment.

Introduction

This *Handbook for Implementing an ISO 14001 Environmental Management System* is designed to provide managers with practical explanations about the structure and implementation of an environmental management system (EMS). To clarify and illustrate this process, we have incorporated the comments and best practices of managers from six different organizations that have implemented an EMS. Four of these organizations have gone on to achieve certification to ISO 14001.

The industries represented here are varied in function and size, ranging from a company with 22 employees that manufactures screw machine products, to an international health care products and services company with 55,000 employees, and to a major seaport with 287,000 employees. As we describe the implementation steps of an ISO 14001 EMS, the companies offer suggestions for meshing each phase with business strategies and drawing employees into the EMS process.

Direct quotes from managers at these organizations let you know how they dealt with a particular element of the standard. In addition, practical advice from our contributors is presented in highlighted text boxes.

We assume that you, our readers, are managers or technical staff with some knowledge of environmental protection practices, or that you work closely with environmental staff.

Organizations that embrace the principles of the ISO 14001 standard can expect to reap the benefits of systematically managing environmental liabilities and challenges. Historically, the Plan-Do-Check-Act cycle—the basis for ISO 14001—has resulted in cost savings, improved sales, more efficient processes, and more satisfied customers for organizations. ISO 14001 is now becoming an indicator of environmental responsibility and superior environmental performance among companies.

How to Use This Handbook

This handbook provides step-by-step instructions for practical implementation of an ISO 14001 EMS. In these pages, you can learn how to identify environmental aspects and impacts, establish objectives and targets, and how to document processes and procedures. Training, teambuilding, and communication are also clearly defined. Chapters 1 through 3 provide background information. Skip these chapters if you are familiar with EMSs and ISO 14001 and go directly to Chapter 4.

Many environmental managers have told us that they found the format of the First Edition easy to work with and jotted down notes on the blank pages and in the margins. We encourage you to do the same and, to make it easier, we have provided a Notes section at the end of each chapter.

NOTE: You should plan to have a copy of the ISO 14001 standard on hand to receive the maximum benefit of this handbook. Appendix B provides information about where to purchase a copy if you do not have one. ■

Notes

Introduction

Employees take pride in being a part of the EMS implementation process.

Chapter One
Environmental Management Systems

Historically, organizations have managed their environmental challenges in response to external pressure from governmental agencies, environmental interest groups, and citizens. The focus has been on regulatory compliance—an absence of notices of violation was considered a measure of success. The need to comply with environmental regulations was seen as an additional cost to business that reduced a company's ability to grow and to create new jobs.

> **If You Care About Our Environment, Please Don't Throw In The Towel.**
> To help protect our environment, Coast Hotels & Resorts is implementing a Towel Saver Program. In doing this we hope to help reduce the amount of laundry detergent being released into our waterways. If you would like your towels changed, please drop them into the bathtub or shower. If you do not require fresh towels, simply return them to the towel rack.
> Thank-you for your support.
> **Coast Hotels & Resorts**

Now, companies recognize that sound environmental management results in economic gain. As part of their environmental management, eighteen Veterans Affairs medical centers received Energy Star® awards in May 2003 for their energy efficiency. The joint Environmental Protection Agency (EPA)/Department of Energy (DOE) Energy Star® program applies to buildings within the top 25 percent in the nation in energy efficiency. *GreenBiz.com* for May 27, 2003 reports that these awards support President Bush's National Energy Policy, which calls on DOE to "extend the Department of Energy's Energy Star efficiency program to include schools, retail buildings, health care facilities, and homes."

The Shanghai Daily's eastday.com reports in its May 27, 2003 issue that Shanghai's environmental protection industry has grown rapidly, at a rate of 20 percent a year, with total output reaching 10.4 billion yuan (US$1.25 billion). According to the Shanghai Environmental Protection Bureau, the city has an average of nearly 60,000 tons of industrial, commercial, and household garbage daily, as well as 5,000,000 tons of wastewater. Shanghai is focusing on the equipment market for environmental protection, manufacturing equipment to deal with wastewater, garbage, and the atmosphere. *Eastday.com* states that ISO 14001 has become "a hot property among local companies, with nearly 50 companies joining the system."

In addition to upgrading their energy efficiency and waste treatment and control technologies, companies recognize that environmental management has become an integral part of doing business. Their environmental programs are more efficient, effective, and responsive through the implementation of an environmental management system, or EMS.

Environmentally Friendly Vehicles

GreenBiz.com reports in its March 14, 2003 online newsletter that the American Council for an Energy-Efficient Economy (ACEEE) has released its 2003 edition of *ACEEE's Green Book®: The Environmental Guide to Cars & Trucks*. This book lists environmentally friendly passenger cars, trucks, and SUVs. Each car's "Green Score" evaluates vehicles for consumers on a basis of fuel consumption and air pollution, including both unhealthy tailpipe emissions and the emissions of gases that cause global warming.

Green Cars and Trucks

"America's car-buying decisions have significant energy, economic, and environmental impacts," said Bill Prindle, deputy director of ACEEE. "If new car and light truck buyers chose the most efficient vehicles in each size class, we would slash the 2003 fleet's gasoline use by 20 percent, reducing gasoline costs by $3.7 billion, and saving the average buyer $200 a year. And of course, we would also cut greenhouse gas emissions and reduce our dependence on imported oil."

Toyota had 22 cars, trucks, minivans, and SUVs listed in the 2003 Green Book, and has been involved in fuel cell technology development since 1992. The company began testing its Fuel Cell Hybrid Vehicle (FCHV-4) on public roads in 2001, with more than 1,000 on the road by 2003.

Defining an EMS

A management system is the combination of steps an organization takes to manage its processes and activities. An environmental management system, or EMS, is a well-defined management structure designed to address the impacts of an organization's activities, products, and services on the environment.

The Plan-Do-Check-Act cycle that is the foundation of all management systems is the basis of an EMS. The organization needs to have a ***plan*** with clearly defined environmental goals that describe what will be accomplished and the associated time frames. The organization must then implement or ***do*** what is required to carry out the plan, involving the entire organization. A ***check*** of progress in meeting the established goals allows the organization to determine the effectiveness of its plan. Finally, the organization must ***act*** to improve the plan, as this is critical to the success and continued improvement of the EMS.

An EMS provides a consistent approach by clearly defining the management system structure, the assignment of resources and responsibilities, and the regular evaluation of environmental performance. Use of an EMS allows an organization to satisfy environmental performance expectations, control costs, and ensure compliance with regulations.

> ### EMS Provides Consistency for Baxter Operations
>
> *While the likelihood of disparate EMS programs exists with operations in so many countries, Mike Cycyota, director of corporate EHS audits, says that the process is the same at all the Baxter International facilities. "You get your people together, you train them, you identify all of the aspects, and then you rank and manage impacts," he explains. "Environmental regulations in Cartago, Costa Rica are minimal compared to the United States, but the environmental concerns about certain operations are very similar. For example, if there is a solvent-bonding operation in Costa Rica, and another in Aibonito, Puerto Rico, the concerns are the same regarding handling of waste, industrial hygiene issues for exposures, and ergonomics." How these are dealt with may vary, he explains, but this is an individual facility issue rather than a country issue.*

Why implement an EMS?

The primary objective of an EMS is to reduce the impact of an organization's activities, products, and services on the environment. However, this in itself is not a sufficient reason for management to invest the time, effort, and costs in establishing and maintaining an EMS. The organization needs to know that tangible benefits will be returned from its investment. Some measured benefits of implementing an EMS include:

- Improved compliance with environmental regulations.

- Reduced cost of waste management.
- Savings in consumption of energy and materials.
- Improved corporate image among regulators, customers, and the public.
- Reduced costs through cost allocation and process improvements.
- Reduced risk and liabilities.

Companies that have an EMS certified to the ISO 14001 standard recognize benefits to their employees who develop pride in the company's environmental performance as a by-product of implementation. Employees across all functions and levels are involved in the implementation process, learning more about the company and control of environmental aspects, and becoming involved in environmental awareness and training activities.

Demonstrating Environmental Responsibility

"In North America and the European Union, our customers have a great interest in knowing that our products are manufactured in an environmentally responsible manner," Allan Ricketts of Trus Joist, a Weyerhaeuser company, explains. "As a leader in the manufacturing of engineered lumber products, we are committed to developing an environmental management system that is capable of being certified to ISO 14001 to demonstrate our commitment to the process, and demonstrates this commitment to our customers in a clear and direct manner. If our customers request "third party" certification to ISO 14001, we will assess the benefits and cost of certification with the customer, and make a business decision about certification of a manufacturing plant. Our customers have responded positively to our EMS initiative. We constantly seek opportunities to demonstrate our commitment to safely manufacturing the highest quality engineered lumber products in an environmentally responsible manner."

Toyota's ISO 14001 EMS

Toyota put energy and ingenuity into its environmental management system (EMS), implementing the ISO 14001 standard at all its plants, and assessing the aspects of its suppliers through its Green Supplier Guidelines program. All Toyota suppliers must become certified to ISO 14001 by the end of 2003. The company set five-year goals to minimize: energy use; hazardous waste disposed at landfills; water consumption; and emissions of greenhouse gases, volatile organic compounds (VOCs), and toxic chemicals. One example of the effectiveness of the EMS is that Toyota was able to reduce its VOC emissions from body painting by 33 percent in five years by using new materials and technology, as well as improved process controls.

According to Toyota's web site, 75 to 80 percent by weight of each end-of-life Toyota vehicle is reused or recycled, in keeping with legislative initiatives in Europe and Japan that have inspired automakers to improve the recyclability of their vehicles. Toyota's worldwide goal is to have its vehicles be 95 percent recyclable by 2015. Both the European countries and some states and provinces in North America also require reduction or elimination of substances of concern (SOCs), such as mercury, hexavalent chrome, lead, and cadmium, in vehicles to assure safe recycling for end-of-life vehicles.

Because each employee must know and understand the impact of individual activities on the environment, a collective sense of ownership and leadership often emerges. One company stated that recycling, for example, was more than a part of the company's processes, as it was also addressed by the municipality. With so much reinforcement of recycling, employees found this a natural starting point for EMS activity to take off in the organization. Because recycling is also low-risk, it could only have positive benefits. The company found that recycling saved money and materials, and allowed people to feel good about participating, while moving them into resource reduction through a reduce and reuse mode. ■

Recommendations to Others

"Go for it!" Ricardo Valverde, Manager, Environmental Safety and Health, advises, in speaking of his experience at the Baxter plant in Cartago, Costa Rica. "Even if you don't have regulatory or market pressures, the certification will give your company a good name. If you are one of the first organizations in your region to become certified—as the Baxter facility in Costa Rica was—it will be hard to make comparisons with other certified companies. Find another company that is certified to the standard and talk to them."

"I encourage people to come here for a tour," he states. *"Part of the concept of being a leader is to encourage others to follow. As more companies become certified to ISO 14001, the environment gets better. You have to make an investment of money and human resources to become certified, but money can be saved by controlling waste and making other processes more efficient.."*

Notes

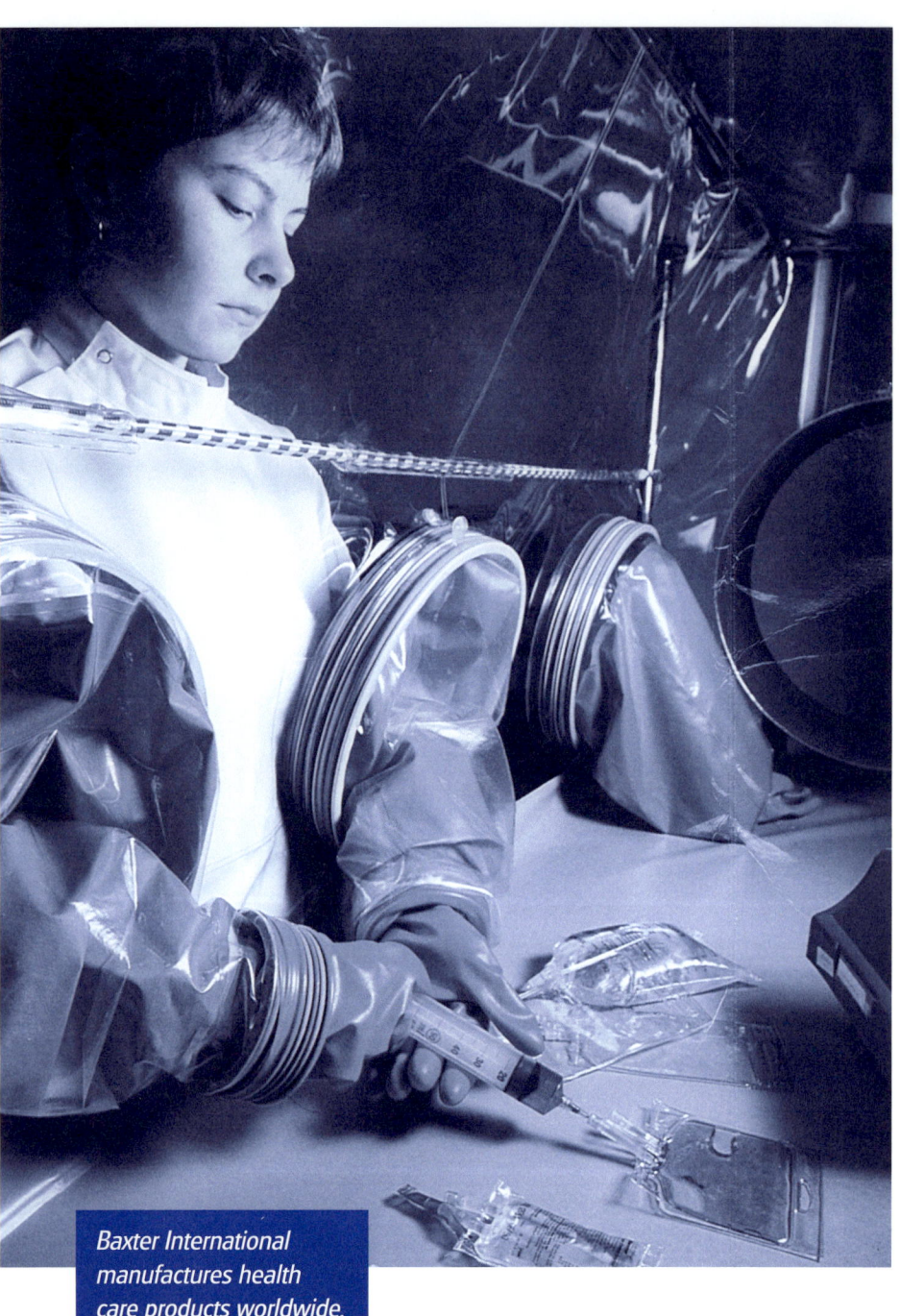

Baxter International manufactures health care products worldwide.

2

Chapter 2
Companies That Have Benefited from an EMS

To learn how companies of various sizes and industries have benefited from environmental management systems, the authors contacted managers at six organizations. These managers provided first-hand insights into the implementation and operation of a successful EMS throughout the handbook.

Baxter International is a major producer, developer, and distributor of health care products and services, with 55,000 employees and sales of more than $8.1 billion in 2002. The company has plants in more than 40 countries in North America, South America, Asia, and Europe, and offers its products to health care providers in more than 100 countries.

Baxter facilities in Ireland

Mike Cycyota, director of corporate EHS audits for Baxter, explains that the previous in-house BEHSt standard that prepared sites for ISO 14001 was sunsetted at the end of 2002. In addition to ISO 14001 certification at most manufacturing and distribution facilities, Baxter is launching implementation of the OHSAS 18001 standard for safety and health effective in 2003. This standard's numbering and format matches that of ISO 14001. Sites will decide individually whether to become certified to OHSAS 18001.

ISO 14001 Simplifies Bids

Mike Cycyota of Baxter notes that being certified to ISO 14001 made it easier to tender bids, especially in the Scandinavian countries. "They had very fragile environments to protect," he explains. "Our Sao Paulo, Brazil facility now finds that customers ask to see the updated ISO 14001 certification, and it has also become very important in China and Japan. Customers assume we have the certification if we claim to be a company that is concerned about the environment. The certification also cuts through a lot of red tape; if you have it, you just give the certification number. If you don't have it, you have to fill out an extensive questionnaire about your environmental program."

BP Exploration Alaska, Inc. explores for and produces oil and gas at five fields (assets) on the North Slope of Alaska and one on the Kenai Peninsula. During 2002, BP had about 1,400 employees and 3,700 contractor personnel supporting its Alaskan activities. BP also holds a 50 percent interest in the Trans-Alaska Pipeline. The characteristics of the company's operations are unique in that the staff is dispersed over a wide geographic area, with contractors as a significant portion of the workforce. Both contractors and employees work rotating shifts, with primarily two-week shifts, as well as rotations among contractors. The Arctic weather presents very harsh working conditions. BP operations have high visibility at a state and national level, with extremely stringent permitting. The company's activities are covered by more than 1,000 permits, 800 of which are currently active. Each permit contains scores of individual stipulations.

Norman Ingram is manager of compliance assurance and continual improvement for BP assets in Alaska. He explains that BP has a corporate mandate for all assets (each asset is an oil field with drilling rigs, processing facilities, and supporting infrastructure) to have an EMS in place that is certified to ISO 14001. The Alaska assets first became certified in 1998, with the number increasing following the Arco merger to eight under one certification.

BP found development and implementation of an ISO 14001 EMS to be value-added, and discovered that it raised the company's environmental performance to a new level. Norman Ingram points out that BP gained increased clarity, discipline, and efficiency, and learned to proactively manage environmental issues instead of reacting to them. He states that having consistent environmental management systems among all BP assets eliminated duplication of efforts in the business units. Another advantage of the ISO 14001 EMS cited by Ingram included finding ways to reduce the amount of waste created, which, in turn, led to reduced pollution and reduced costs for handling, managing, and disposing of waste.

BP's Endicott Oil Field is a man-made island in the Beaufort Sea, north of Alaska.

An EMS Provides Focus

Norman Ingram of BP states that having an EMS gives the company a consistency of environmental management that extends across all business units. Having all sites certified to ISO 14001 worldwide also gives employees a common language to talk about problems, which, in turn, leads to a best practices approach to find the most effective ways to improve performance. "An EMS creates the mechanism that allows us to focus on the most important issues," he states. "In doing this along with targeting improvements and measuring results, improved environmental performance is achieved. The structure of an EMS that conforms to ISO 14001 ensures that you are covering everything from A to Z of the issues; from what's in scope, to policy, to checking. Everything is tied together, and nothing is missing."

Milan Screw Products, Inc. in Milan, Michigan has 22 employees and had annual sales of $2.6 million in 2002 for screw machine products made from steel bars. Its market is about 80 percent fluid power industry and 20 percent automotive and other. Products for the fluid power industry consist of fittings that go on the ends of hydraulic hoses for many kinds of heavy machinery, such as farm equipment and road graders. Milan is certified to ISO 9001:2000, and has an ISO 14001 EMS, but is not certified to the standard. Owner and general manager Chuck Tellas explains that the company may become certified to the standard if the EPA provides some regulatory relief.

Because of the economic downturn in 2003, Milan had to downsize and lost its ISO 14001 champion, but still maintains its EMS. Chuck Tellas says that he plans to do more training and ramp up work with the EMS as the economy recovers. The company's move from a 14,000-square-foot plant to a new 34,000-square-foot plant a few years ago continues to provide opportunities to upgrade its EMS through design and engineering changes.

The Port of Houston is home to a $15 billion petrochemical complex, the largest in the U.S. and second largest in the world, and is a port for more than 100 steamship lines that provide service to 200 ports worldwide. Approximately 194 million tons of cargo passed through its 50-mile-long ship canal in 2001 that was loaded or unloaded at private wharves and at 43 general cargo wharves and two liquid cargo wharves for public hire. Some of the cargo handled at this public port includes computers, wine, televisions, running shoes, large pieces of steel, and grain. Jobs associated with port activity include 287,454 in Texas and 714,000 nationwide, of which 89,710 are direct jobs. Houston became a port for deep-water vessels in 1914. The port's public and private marine terminals generate $10.9 billion per year in business revenues.

Port of Houston

Laura Fiffick, environmental affairs manager for the port, became interested in ISO 14001, and gained management support to become part of an EPA EMS initiative. The Port Authority received its ISO 14001 certification for two facilities, central maintenance and the Barbours Cut Container Terminal, in August 2002. The central maintenance facility supports other facilities for plumbing, air-conditioning, and vehicle and equipment maintenance. The port is committed to being ISO 14001-ready for the Bayport container terminal expansion on the day it opens in fall 2005, adjacent to the Bayport chemical complex.

Trus Joist, a Weyerhaeuser business, was established in 1960 in Boise, Idaho, and is a global leader in the manufacturing and marketing of engineered lumber used in residential, commercial, and industrial construction. Some of these applications include open-web trusses, silent floor joists, and laminated veneer lumber for use in flanges. All the products developed are based on manufacturing technologies to transform wood fiber from fast-growing small diameter trees into high-performance products. The company has 4,000 employees in 21 manufacturing facilities in the United States, Canada, Australia, and the European Union. The company markets engineered lumber in those countries, and is developing emergent markets in Japan, Korea, and China.

Trus Joist's Lowndes County plant in Valdosta, Georgia became certified to ISO 14001 in June 2001. Sixteen Trus Joist plants in the United States and Canada have developed and implemented environmental management systems modeled on the first EMS at the Lowndes Plant. These plants have earned "certification ready" status to ISO 14001 by completing comprehensive certification readiness audits. Three plants that were aligned under Trus Joist when Weyerhaeuser Company acquired the former Willamette Industries have begun developing and implementing EMSs. These plants are scheduled to achieve "certification ready" status to ISO 14001 by October 2004. Allan Ricketts is the Trus Joist Manufacturing Operations Project Manager and has responsibility for safety, quality, and environmental management systems. He is also responsible for process reliability and the Sustainable Forestry Initiative® in log procurement operations.

The U.S. Army, Ft. Lewis, Washington, public works department became certified to ISO 14001 on September 5, 2000. The public works group includes real property maintenance operations, such as building maintenance, boilers, electricity, construction, fire department, and environmental, and is made up of 450 government and contract personnel. The base itself comprises 86,000 acres inhabited by 21,000 military personnel, 5,000 civilian personnel, and 9,700 family members.

Paul Steucke, chief of the environmental and natural resources division, states that the public works department at Ft. Lewis has always had a progressive environmental program, winning an award in 1985 for environmental quality and performance. ISO 14001 became a standard at about the time public works wanted to move its program to a proactive rather than reactive level. His group joined a Department of Defense (DOD) wide pilot study from January 1998 to January 2000 for organizations that wanted to implement ISO 14001 to evaluate the standard in military applications. ∎

ISO 14001 Makes Sense

Paul Steucke's first barrier was getting the leadership of public works at Ft. Lewis interested from a competitive standpoint, and educated about how ISO 14001 works. "The beauty of ISO 14001 is that it makes sense. A lot of it has to do with doing things you should be doing anyway. There is nothing wrong with having key documents controlled and having standard operating procedures, and having procedures in place to see if your processes are working properly. Opposing the concept of continual improvement is like arguing against motherhood and apple pie."

Bankcards are standardized for magnetic strip data content and coded character sets, allowing the cards to be used worldwide (ISO 4909).

Chapter 3
The Evolution of International Management System Standards

As of December 31, 2002, more than 13,736 international standards have been developed and published by members of the International Organization for Standardization. The organization was founded in 1947. Headquartered in Geneva, Switzerland, its members from 146 countries are dedicated to promoting standardization of manufacturing and communications to simplify international trade. Funding is provided through memberships and sales of standards and publications. A member body of ISO is the national body "most representative of standardization in its country," with one organization in each country accepted for membership. Examples of national bodies include:

- United States: ANSI - American National Standards Institute
- United Kingdom: BSI - British Standards Institution
- Germany: DIN - Deutsches Institut fur Normung
- Canada: SCC - Standards Council of Canada

Milan Screw Products

How ISO Standards Are Developed

More than 2,937 technical committees, subcommittees, and working groups develop ISO standards that are later submitted as draft international standards. Once the technical aspects of the standard are agreed upon, the draft of the proposed standard must be approved by two-thirds of those involved in its development, plus 75 percent of all voting members. The agreed-upon text is then published as an ISO International Standard. These voluntary standards are used to ensure that materials, products, processes, and services are suitable for their intended use. Some examples of the kinds of things ISO standards cover are:

- *Bankcards* are standardized for magnetic strip data content and coded character sets, allowing the cards to be used worldwide (ISO 4909).
- *Ropes* are defined as to size, types of construction, minimum breaking load, and linear mass. ISO 1346 applies to polypropylene ropes, while ISO 2020 is for preformed flexible steel wire rope for aircraft controls.
- *Screw threads* are defined by ISO 68 and related standards to eliminate inconsistencies of size and design that result in maintenance problems, when lost or damaged nuts or bolts cannot easily be replaced.
- *Symbols for Automobile Controls* are defined in ISO 2575 so the same displays for controls appear in cars all over the world.

ISO 9000 Quality Management Standards Emerge

In 1987, the ISO 9000 quality management system standards were issued in response to the need for a uniform quality management system standard. Although initial interest in the standards was low-key, this interest later became very intense, leading to swift, widespread adoption of ISO 9000. Certification to this series of standards became a prerequisite for trade in many regions. At the end of 2001, a staggering 510,616 organizations had received ISO 9000 certification.

The 1994 ISO 9000 series included three conformance standards: ISO 9001, ISO 9002, and ISO 9003. In 2000, these were merged into a single standard, ISO 9001:2000, to correspond with the elements and processes of ISO 14001. An organization may become certified (registered) to the standard. ISO 9004 is a set of guidelines that provides performance improvement recommendations for organizations that are developing a quality management system. ISO 9000 lists the fundamentals and vocabulary for quality management systems.

Companies become certified following a quality system audit by an ISO 9001:2000-accredited registrar who audits and monitors quality management systems. After the initial certification, the registrar periodically performs audits to determine whether the company is maintaining and improving its performance as required by the standard.

ISO 14000 Environmental Management Standards Evolve

In 1991, with the acceptance of ISO 9000 and of business systems in general, and a greater public awareness of environmental issues, the International Organization for Standardization began to research the need for environmental management standards. The goals of the environmental management standards are to:

- Promote a common approach to environmental management on a par with the quality management standards.
- Enhance the ability of organizations to attain and measure environmental performance.
- Facilitate trade and remove trade barriers.

The ISO 14000 environmental management standards were developed to provide a framework that organizations can use to measure and monitor environmental issues in a consistent way. In addition, a growing general awareness emerged that sound environmental management makes good business sense.

ISO 14000 is a series of voluntary environmental standards and guidelines that were developed to promote more uniform and effective environmental management worldwide. These standards either address the environmental impacts of the organization, or the environmental impacts of products and processes. See Figures 3-1 and 3-2.

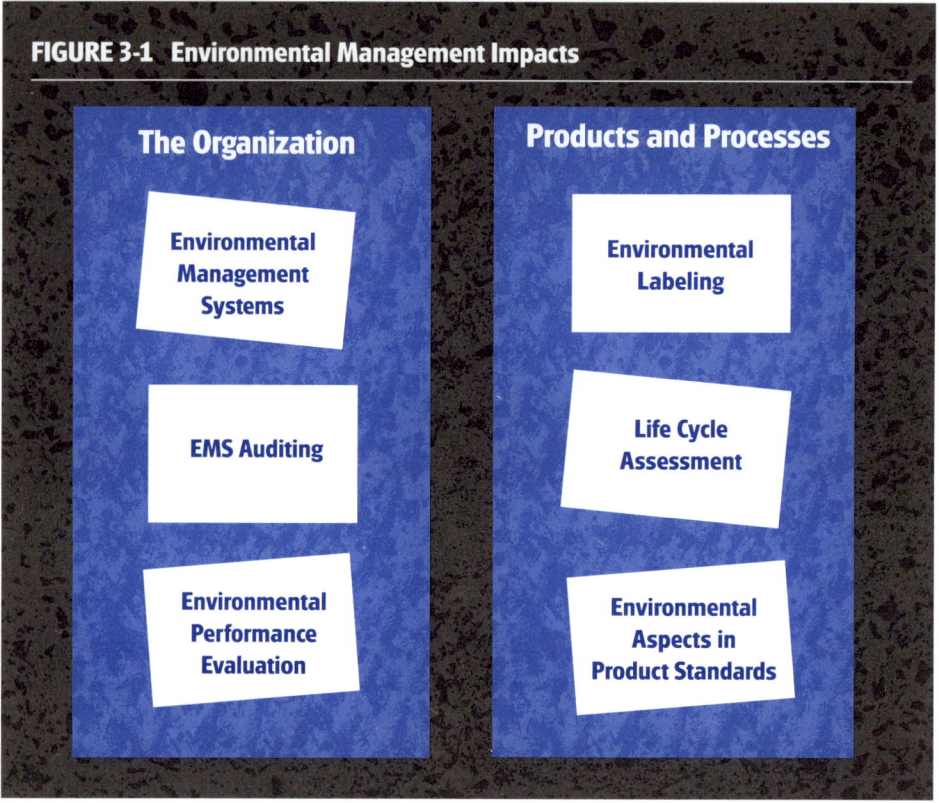

FIGURE 3-2 ISO 14000 Environmental Management Standards

Standard/Guideline	Title
ISO 14001	Environmental Management Systems—Specification with Guidance for Use
ISO 14004	Environmental Management Systems—General Guidelines on Principles, Systems, and Supporting Techniques
ISO 14015	Environmental Management—Environmental Assessment of Site and Organizations
ISO 14020	Environmental Labels and Declarations—General Principles
ISO 14021-14023	Environmental Labels and Declarations—Self Declared Environmental Claims (Type II)
ISO 14024	Environmental Labels and Declarations—Type I Environmental Labeling—Principles and Procedures
ISO 14025	Environmental Labels and Declarations—Type III Environmental Declarations
ISO/TR 14032:1999	Environmental Management—Examples of Environmental Performance Evaluation (EPE)
ISO 14031	Environmental Management—Environmental Performance Evaluation—Guidelines
ISO 14040	Environmental Management—Life Cycle Assessment—Principles and Framework
ISO 14041	Environmental Management—Life Cycle Assessment—Goal and Scope Definition and Inventory Analysis
ISO 14042	Environmental Management—Life Cycle Assessment—Life Cycle Impact Assessment
ISO 14043	Environmental Management—Life Cycle Assessment—Life Cycle Interpretation
ISO/TR 14047	Environmental Management—Life Cycle Assessment—Examples of Application of ISO 14042
ISO/TR 14049:2000	Environmental Management—Life Cycle Assessment—Examples of Application of ISO 14041 to Goal and Scope Definition and Inventory Analysis
ISO 14050:2002	Environmental Management—Vocabulary
ISO/TR 14062:2002	Environmental Management—Integrating Environmental Aspects into Product Design and Development
ISO/AWI 14064	Guidelines for Measuring, Reporting, and Verifying Entity Project-level Greenhouse Gas Emissions
ISO 19011:2002	Guidelines for Quality and/or Environmental Management Systems Auditing (This standard replaces ISO 14010, 14011, and 14012.)
ISO Guide 64: 1997	Guide for the Inclusion of Environmental Aspects in Product Standards
ISO/IEC Guide 66	General Requirements for Bodies Operating Assessment and Certification/Registration of Environmental Management Systems (EMS)

The Organization

Environmental Management System (ISO 14001 and 14004)

An organization's EMS, auditing, and environmental performance evaluation define how the organization manages environmental risks. The EMS allows the organization to meet its environmental obligations as consistently and reliably as it meets manufacturing and financial obligations.

The ISO 14001 standard describes the basic requirements of an EMS. Each organization can expand upon these basic requirements by adding its own company-specific requirements. ISO 14001, which has five main components, is the only standard of the ISO 14000 series to which an organization can be certified (registered) by an independent third party. ISO 14004 provides information and guidance on developing an EMS. By the end of 2001, 36,765 organizations had been certified to ISO 14001.

Environmental Management Systems Auditing (ISO 19011:2002)

An EMS must be audited to evaluate its performance. Unlike an environmental compliance audit that is performed to check for compliance with environmental regulations, the EMS audit checks for conformance to ISO 14001 and to the organization's policies and procedures.

It is important that the EMS be designed to work for the users, not to create paperwork for the auditors. Auditors rely upon representative sampling to determine the effectiveness of the EMS, and can provide valuable feedback about the system. Audits are performed by both in-house (internal) auditors and by third-party (external) auditors. The ISO 19011 EMS auditing standard explains the principles of EMS auditing, procedures for conducting EMS audits, and criteria for evaluating the qualifications of environmental management system auditors.

NOTE: ISO 19011, issued in the fall of 2002, applies to auditing of both quality and environmental management systems, and replaces ISO 14010, 14011, and 14012.

Environmental Performance Evaluation (ISO 14031 – 14032)

The objectives and targets that an organization sets are based on its significant environmental aspects and regulatory requirements. ISO 14001 does not specify performance levels for objectives and targets, such as 10 percent reduction in air emissions or a two-fold reduction in biological oxygen demand levels in wastewater effluent. For this reason, the environmental performance evaluation standard was created to help managers establish a process to measure EMS performance.

The process of environmental performance evaluation identifies and quantifies the impact that a company has on the environment. Measurements of resulting improvements are evaluated against baseline levels. This standard is an aid to setting EMS performance metrics, and is not required for ISO 14001 certification.

Products and Processes

The environmental benefits of a product in terms of its packaging, content, use and disposal are often proclaimed on the product's label. Paper and plastic products, for example, commonly have labels (known as ecolabels) identifying them as recyclable.

The phases of a product's life, from raw material through manufacture, use, and disposal are referred to as the product's life cycle. The ISO 14000 ecolabeling and life-cycle standards provide uniformity for the use of ecolabels and the processes for measuring a product's life cycle.

Environmental Labeling (ISO 14020 – 14025)

The International Organization for Standardization has identified three types of labels: Type I, Type II, and Type III.

Type I Labels: Third Party Environmental Labeling Programs

Issued by independent third party organizations, such as Green Cross, Green Seal (United States), Blue Angel (Germany), and Nordic Swan (Scandinavia); Type I labels are for products that have been independently tested and certified as having met specific environmental criteria.

Type II Labels: Self-Declaration Environmental Claims

A Type II label indicates that the manufacturer makes environmental claims for its products without third-party verification. The Möbius Loop for recycling is a universally recognized Type II ecolabel. The Type II standard establishes guidelines for environmental claims and rules for the use of specific terms and symbols. For example, the standard defines recyclable, compostable, and reduced resource use, and provides guidance for the use of the Möbius Loop.

Type III Labels: Environmental Information Profiles

These labels—which are still being developed and are comparable to nutritional labels on food products—document a product's environmental sustainability, or ability to be produced without harm to the environment.

Life-Cycle Assessment (ISO 14040 – 14049)

Life-Cycle Assessment (LCA) provides a means for determining the impacts that products being manufactured by a company have on today's environment, as well as that of future generations. This assessment evaluates impacts that occur during the entire life cycle of the product that extends from the acquisition of raw materials, to manufacturing, use, and ultimate disposal. The ISO Life Cycle standards cover the four phases of LCA:

1. *Goal definition and scoping* identifies the purpose of the study and the means for attaining the goal. LCAs are usually individual case studies.
2. *Inventory analysis* identifies and quantifies the inputs (raw materials, energy) and outputs (products, wastes) of a product system. See Figure 3-3.
3. *Impact assessment* identifies the environmental impacts of the inputs and outputs.

FIGURE 3-3 Product Life Cycle

INPUTS	PRODUCT LIFE CYCLE	OUTPUTS
Energy	Raw materials acquisition	Water effluents
Raw materials	Manufacturing	Airborne emissions
	Distribution and transportation	Solid wastes
	Use/reuse maintenance	environmental releases
	Recycle	Usable products
	Waste management	

4. *Interpretation* is evaluation of the relative severity of the impacts to allow a decision to be made.

Vocabulary (ISO 14050)

This guide provides a listing of the terms and definitions used throughout all the ISO 14000 standards.

Environmental Aspects in Product Standards (ISO Guide 64)

When the majority of ISO standards were developed, technical committees had specific products in mind. For this reason, the international committee making these determinations agreed to issue ISO Guide 64 that evaluates the environmental impact of the development of a new standard. An instrument calibration standard, for example, may require the use of a calibration gas containing hydrofluorocarbons that contribute to global warming. This standard would require that a more environmentally benign gas be selected.

Government Agencies Take Note of ISO 14000

The ISO 14000 standards are important because federal environmental regulatory agencies, such as the U.S. EPA and Environment Canada, and state and provincial regulatory agencies are involved in evaluating their effectiveness. Other organizations that place an emphasis on environmental management standards include:

The U.S. Securities and Exchange Commission requires publicly traded companies to report environmental liabilities on their balance sheets. Companies with well-run environmental programs often have a stock performance that is above other companies in their industry sector.

The U.S. Federal Trade Commission has issued a series of guidelines for companies to follow when making claims about the environmental attributes of products or packages in connection with the sale or marketing of such items for personal, commercial, institutional, or industrial use.

The U.S. Department of Justice has issued guidelines for setting sentences for environmental crimes. Mitigating factors that can reduce penalties include a commitment to environmental compliance, willingness to report known violations, and a lack of intent to damage the environment. The organization can demonstrate this commitment through the integration of environmental policies and procedures into business operations and a system to audit its environmental compliance, both of which are central to an ISO 14001 EMS.

The U.S. Departments of Energy and Defense are adopting ISO 14001 at facilities throughout the United States.

The European Union has had the Environmental Management and Audit Scheme (EMAS) in place for several years. EMAS is similar to ISO 14001, with the further requirement that the organization issue an annual environmental report describing its impacts on the environment and its programs designed to limit these impacts. ∎

Notes

Operations that have an impact on the environment will need documented procedures.

Chapter 4
Structure of ISO 14001

onfiguration of the Standard

An EMS that conforms to ISO 14001 provides a consistent and systematic framework for improved environmental performance that involves employees in all departments and at all levels. To achieve this goal, ISO 14001 requires:

- Writing an environmental policy.
- Setting environmental objectives and targets.
- Implementing the EMS through training, documentation, and procedures.
- Checking progress.
- Reviewing overall system performance.

Through implementation of the EMS, these components are integrated into a cohesive system. The standard configures these parts of an EMS into a standard format that includes four clauses and three annexes. These are described below.

1. Scope

The scope of the standard presents the key elements of an EMS. Having these elements in place makes it possible for an organization to systematically manage the impacts of its operations on the environment. The scope does not set levels of environmental performance, such as requiring that water or air emissions be below specific levels or concentrations, nor does it establish predetermined levels of waste reduction within a prescribed timeframe.

The difference between having a management system to address environmental challenges versus just meeting regulatory compliance is an important distinction. A lack of clarity about the function of an EMS has resulted in skepticism by those who view the ISO 14001 standard as not having any "legal teeth." It is important to understand that the organization must commit to regulatory compliance as a basic requirement of ISO 14001.

2. Normative References

This section is set aside for cross-references to other documents, none of which exist at present.

3. Definitions

The definitions section is a glossary of terms used throughout the standard. Reading and understanding these definitions is a prerequisite to understanding how the EMS works. Among these, there are three important key definitions for environment, environmental aspect, and environmental impact.

Environment is defined as the *"surroundings in which an organization operates, including air, water, land, natural resources, flora, fauna, and humans, and their interrelation."*

Trus Joist harvests small diameter trees that grow quickly.

Intentionally very broad, this term does not limit the environment to elements that are regulated, nor does it exclude humans from the environment. Because of this broader application, health and safety issues can be incorporated into the EMS without specifically being required by the standard.

Environmental aspect is an *"element of an organization's activities, products, or services that can interact with the environment."*

The identification of an organization's environmental aspects is at the heart of the EMS, so these can be managed and controlled. The planning phase of the EMS involves the process of aspect identification.

Environmental impact is *"any change to the environment, whether adverse or beneficial, wholly or partially resulting from an organization's activities, products, or services."*

Significant environmental aspects of your operations are identified during the planning phase of the EMS. A significant aspect is one that can have potentially significant environmental impacts. By focusing on the significant aspects in your organization, it is possible to attain the greatest improvements. After substantive issues have been addressed, you can then deal with the less significant environmental aspects of operations. As your EMS matures and the system is optimized, the relative gains will be less substantial.

4. Environmental Management System Requirements

This section, the standard proper, consists of six main elements. Explanations of these elements and their applications to your organization are addressed in the following chapters of this handbook. These elements are:

4.1 General Requirements

4.2 Environmental Policy

4.3 Planning

4.4 Implementation and Operation

4.5 Checking and Corrective Action

4.6 Management Review

Notice that the standard's management system is based on the Plan-Do-Check-Act model.

Annex A. Guidance on the Use of the Specification

Annex A was developed to clarify elements of the standard. Each element is cross-referenced in Annex A, using the same numbering system, (e.g., 4.3.1 Environmental Aspects is addressed under A 4.3.1).

Annex B. Links Between ISO 14001 and ISO 9001

ISO 14001 has many features in common with ISO 9001, such as the requirements for document control, records, corrective and preventive action, system audits, and management review. Annex B is a table cross-referencing these common features between the two standards. This is a useful resource for organizations that are certified to ISO 9001. However, an organization does not need to have ISO 9001 in place to embark upon ISO 14001 implementation.

Note: ISO 9001:2000, the current version, is not referenced in ISO 14001 but has all the common elements of ISO 14001.

Annex C. Bibliography

Annex C is a list of related ISO quality and environmental management standards.

4.1 General Requirements

Element 4.1 of ISO 14001 states that *"the organization shall establish and maintain an environmental management system, the requirements of which are described in the whole of clause 4."*

In other words, all elements of ISO 14001 must be implemented for the EMS to be a fully functioning system. It is not unusual for an organization to believe that it has a system in place when, in fact, it only has only parts of a system. When baseline audits for an EMS are performed, it often occurs that the corrective action and management review elements are poorly developed or nonexistent.

Getting Started

Chapters 5 through 9 explain the required elements of ISO 14001 in detail. As you read and understand the standard, you will need to have a plan to implement your EMS. Figure 4-1 provides a checklist for implementation. ■

FIGURE 4-1   A Checklist for EMS Implementation

1. Establish Project Team.
   - Select representatives from multiple departments.
   - Seek reps with diverse skills.
   - Write a team charter with senior management support.
   - Announce formation of the team and the purpose of the EMS implementation.

2. Prepare EMS Implementation Plan.
   - Identify project objectives.
   - Define project scope.
   - Develop project schedule.
   - Assign resources.
   - Establish a project reporting process.

3. Perform EMS Gap Analysis.
   - Compare current processes to ISO 14001 standard.
   - Identify gaps.
   - Revise EMS implementation plan.

4. Conduct EMS Planning.
   - Identify environmental aspects.
   - Identify significant environmental aspects.
   - Set objectives and targets.
   - Establish environmental management programs.

5. Conduct EMS Training and Awareness Program.
   - Provide general EMS awareness to all employees.
   - Train core team in aspects analysis.
   - Conduct internal auditor training for selected personnel.

Continued on next page

Figure 4-1, continued from previous page

> 6. Check System Implementation.
>   - ☐ Conduct internal audits.
>   - ☐ Initiate corrective actions.
>   - ☐ Conduct management review.
>
> 7. Select Registrar.
>   - ☐ Interview several companies.
>   - ☐ Determine skills and experience of audit team.
>   - ☐ Conduct a pre-assessment audit.
>   - ☐ Conduct the registration audit.
>
> 8. Celebrate!!!

Notes

Notes

BP's EMS includes protection of habitat for local wildlife.

Chapter 5
4.2 Environmental Policy

he Standard Requires...

In ISO 14001 (3.9), the *environmental policy* is defined as a *"statement by the organization of its intentions and principles, in relation to overall environmental performance, which provides a framework for action, and for the setting of environmental objectives and targets."*

The policy must:

- Be initiated and perpetuated through top management commitment.
- Incorporate a commitment to continual improvement and the prevention of pollution.
- Include a commitment to compliance with all applicable regulations.
- Provide a framework for environmental objectives and targets.
- Be documented, implemented, maintained, and communicated to all employees.
- Be available to the public.

The environmental policy is a driver for implementing and improving the environmental management system, which leads to improved environmental performance. To be effective, the policy needs to be clearly understandable to all employees and to present a high-level perspective of the organization's environmental values. Goals and objectives are not specified in the environmental policy.

> ### Environmental Policy is a Management Decision
>
> *Milan General Manager Chuck Tellas sought a strong environmental statement that would not limit the company to specific, measured goals in the policy. Tellas explains that he worked with a consultant in developing the environmental policy. "I felt I had to do this," he points out, "rather than the employees, as this is the policy of the company, not a consensus document. This is what I want to see us accomplish. It took a couple of drafts to get it right, and even then, we went back and changed some of it later."*

It is recommended that the policy be reviewed annually and revised to reflect changing conditions and information within the organization as part of continual improvement.

How to Develop An Environmental Policy

A successful environmental policy must be well *written* and well *communicated*, which is a very demanding part of implementation. Visible and specific communication lets employees know the direction and intent of the organization in pursuing its environmental values so that they may participate and share in this ideology. The requirement of ISO 14001 that the environmental policy be communicated to all employees and made available to the public is a major challenge when considering the amount of information that employees receive daily. The policy must compete with other company policies, procedures, and memos, and may receive no more than a passing notice unless it is issued with a supporting awareness program.

Two Examples of Environmental Policies

Environmental, Health and Safety Policy
Our Commitment to People and the Environment

— Adopted August 4, 1997

Baxter will be a global leader in Environmental, Health and Safety (EHS) management. This is consistent with Baxter's business interests, ethics and shared values.

Specifically, we commit to the following:

Sustainable Development
We will strive to conserve resources and minimize or eliminate adverse EHS effects and risks that may be associated with our products, services and operations.

Employees
We will provide a safe and healthy workplace, striving to prevent injuries and illnesses, promoting healthy lifestyles and encouraging respect for the environment. We will ensure that our employees have the awareness, skills and knowledge to carry out this policy.

Compliance
We will meet all applicable EHS laws and Baxter EHS requirements, including our own EHS management standards.

Business Integration
We will integrate EHS considerations into our business activities.

Customers
We will work with our customers to help them address their EHS needs.

Suppliers and Contractors
We will work with our suppliers and contractors to enhance EHS performance.

Community and Government
We will participate in community and government EHS initiatives.

Baxter commits to continuous improvement in environmental, health and safety performance. We will set goals, measure progress and communicate results. Compliance with this policy is the responsibility of every employee.

Harry M. Jansen Kraemer, Jr.
Chairman and
Chief Executive Officer

William R. Blackburn
Vice President and
Chief Counsel,
Corporate Environment,
Health and Safety

Baxter

Two Examples of Environmental Policies

MILAN SCREW PRODUCTS, INC.
291 Squires Drive P.O. Box 180
Milan, MI 48160

(734) 439-2431   Fax (734) 439-1040

Statement of Corporate Environmental Policy

Milan Screw Products Inc. is committed to continual improvement of its Environmental Management System (EMS), which includes waste minimization, the prevention of pollution, and compliance with all relevant federal, state, and local environmental legislation and regulations. The company will meet or exceed the environmental requirements of other organizations to which Milan Screw Products subscribes. To sustain this commitment, the requirements of the Environmental Management System described in this Manual applies to all activities, equipment, material and employees.

The company's Environmental Compliance Officer is the company's EMS Management Representative who has the responsibility and authority to plan, enforce, and maintain the company's Environmental Management System. This responsibility also includes stoppage of activities that deviate from the requirements of this Manual. The Environmental Compliance Officer, with the assistance of the Environmental Task Group, will propose annual targets and objectives to be approved by the Management Review Board.

The EMS Management Representative may delegate some of this authority downward through the organization in order to effectively implement the system.

Charles Tellas
Charles Tellas
President and CEO

December 10, 1995

action items

Environmental Policy

- Keep it simple.
- Present the policy with training.
- Post it extensively.
- Give copies of the policy to as many people as you can.
- Post the policy on company Internet and intranet sites.
- Print the policy on the backs of employee ID tags.
- Issue the policy to all employees on wallet cards.

One environmental manager, who had over 1,000 copies of a well-written safety and environmental policy printed and sent to all employees, found that a year later, few could recall that it existed. Another company had poster-size copies of the policy printed, framed, and hung throughout its facility, but found, during an EMS audit, that fewer than 40 percent of the employees knew of the policy.

None of these actions will succeed on its own. The policy must become an integral part of an EMS awareness and communication program, explaining the purpose of the policy, its relationship to the EMS, and how the EMS involves everyone. The Port of Houston found that employees weren't retaining the EMS training content, so Laura Fiffick and her core team developed "Environmental Jeopardy." Employees split up into teams and were quizzed about the EMS, with the winning team receiving small prizes. Interest in the EMS increased significantly, and the game helped people remember the training sessions and key EMS facts.

 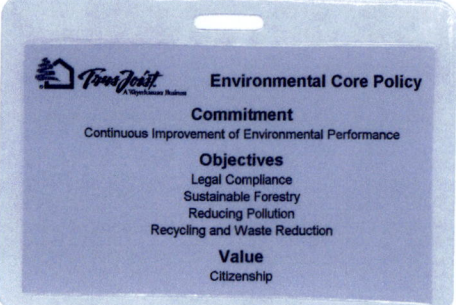

Trus Joist prints the Environmental Core Policy on wallet cards for employees.

Environmental Policy to Go

Trus Joist puts its environmental policy is on its I.D. badges and wallet cards that employees carry when at work. One line of the company's safety policy sums up Trus Joist's safety, quality, sustainable forestry, and environmental values: "Safely manufacture the highest quality engineered lumber products in an environmentally responsible manner to meet our customers' needs."

Trus Joist embraces the Weyerhaeuser Environmental Core Policy that is based on the Weyerhaeuser Value of Citizenship. This core policy establishes specific objectives of legal compliance, sustainable forestry, reducing pollution, recycling and waste management, and confirms a commitment to continual improvement of environmental performance. "Taking Responsibility" is the theme, which summarizes the company's commitment to safely manufacturing the highest quality engineered lumber products in an environmentally responsible manner.

The port inundated employees with information, including "stall talk," posters and placards inside restroom stalls. They had information in the employee newsletter and sent out flyers. They came up with a leaping dolphin for an environmental mascot that was dubbed "The Captain." CAPTAIN is an acronym for Continually Achieving Protection Through Training, Awareness, and Innovation for Natural Resources. When employees see The Captain on a document, they know immediately that it is environmental. Company I.D. badges have The Captain on one side and a list of questions an EMS auditor could ask on the other.

The port also sends out postcards every six months with The Captain and environmental policy on one side and updates about something especially well done on the other. At the port's annual picnic, environmental awards are given out for the best team and individual contributions.

As implementation of an ISO 14001 EMS progresses, the ideology instilled in the policy is demonstrated in the workings of the EMS. Making the policy available to the general public is addressed in greater detail in Chapter 7 under External Communication. ∎

"Let's work together for a clean Port of Houston!"

- Reduce Air Emissions
- Reduce Storm Water Impacts
- Recycle and Minimize Waste
- Reward Effort and Excellence

– The Captain™

Continually
Achieving
Protection through
Training,
Awareness and
Innovation for our
Natural resources

EPA
United States Environmental Protection Agency

A partnership in Environmental Management Systems

All EMS-related internal communications for the Port of Houston carry the jaunty Captain logo.

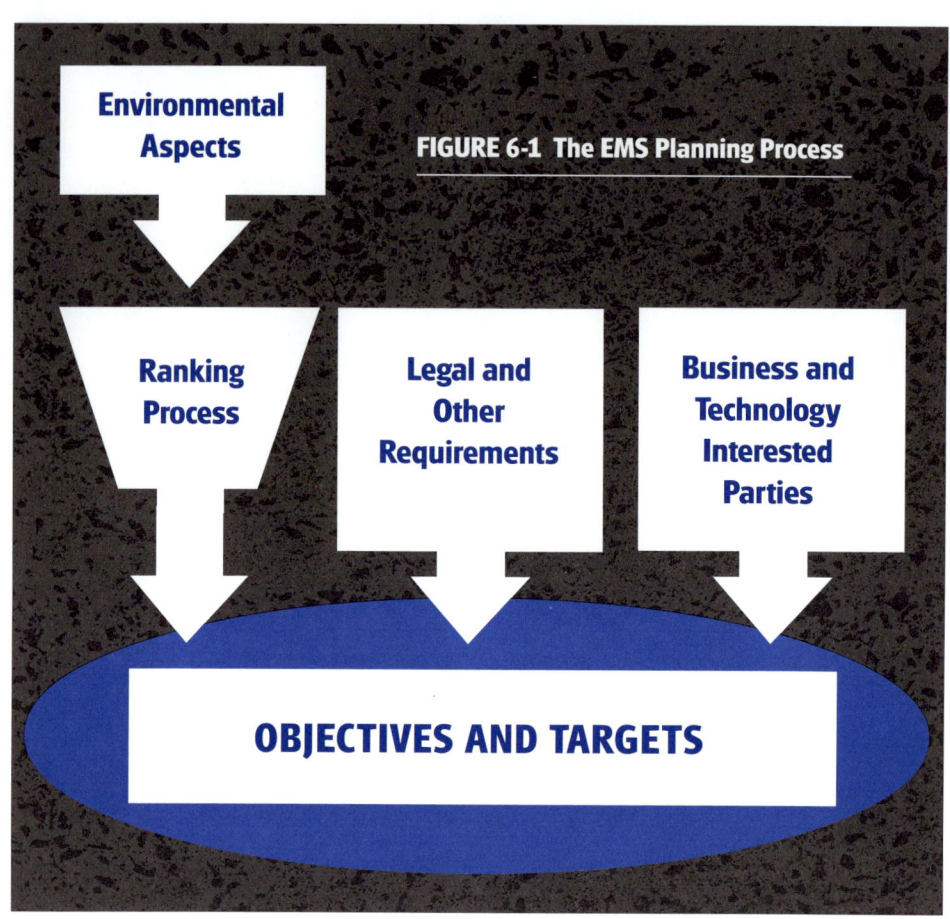

FIGURE 6-1 The EMS Planning Process

Chapter 6
4.3 Planning

he first part of the Plan-Do-Check-Act improvement loop is the *plan* portion.

The Standard Requires...

Element 4.3 of ISO 14001 requires procedures to identify environmental aspects of the organization's activities, products, and services; to identify legal and other requirements; to establish and maintain documented environmental objectives and targets at each relevant function and level; and to establish programs to achieve the objectives and targets.

The overall intent of the EMS planning process is to set achievable and measurable goals (objectives and targets) for the EMS. The objectives and targets are determined by considering a range of factors that include: activities that pose a potentially high risk to the environment (significant aspects), legal obligations, business requirements, technical limitations, and social considerations. Plans (environmental management programs) are written to ensure the objectives and targets are met. These plans identify the budget and schedule needed to meet the goals. Figure 6-1 illustrates the EMS planning process.

Planning the EMS Strategically

Allan Ricketts of Trus Joist advises the EMS core team to keep a few things in mind. "Look for opportunities to integrate your EMS with other management systems you have in place, as this results in significant savings of resources in people, time, and money. You may already have an effective safety or quality management system, some portions of which already meet certain requirements of ISO 14001, such as document and data control, corrective and preventive action, management review, and internal audits and training. Reducing redundancy and effort in the care and feeding of separate management systems can go a long way to getting a good return on this investment in your business. There are two critical steps to get right.

1. *Clearly define and articulate your environmental policy, and drive it across your business. Make sure people clearly understand your business level commitment to the process and define your objectives. Employees must understand the value of an effective EMS to your business. Senior business leaders should continually support and reinforce this commitment.*

2. *Develop a business EMS implementation plan with strategies and operational business leaders' support for implementing and resourcing the plan. I suggest you allocate about 30 percent of the total EMS implementation time to the planning phase. Once planning is complete, you should invest time in communicating and coordinating the implementation plan across your business."*

4.3.1 Environmental Aspects

The EMS reflects the organization's environmental aspects and associated impacts. ISO 14001 defines an environmental aspect as any element of an organization's activities that can interact with the environment. Because all other EMS elements are built upon the evaluation of environmental aspects, the process must be accurate and detailed.

Using a logical and dependable methodology, the EMS team must establish a documented procedure to identify the environmental aspects (and associated impacts) and their relative significance. The ISO 14001 standard does not provide an aspects identification procedure.

Begin evaluation of aspects and impacts by looking at the activities, products, and services performed by your organization. For example, list your company's activities and how they impact the environment.

After environmental aspects have been identified, determine the environmental impacts associated with each aspect. Regulated aspects will be readily identifiable, although it is necessary to look beyond regulatory requirements. Aspects that are not directly regulated include energy and water use, consumption of raw materials, odor, traffic, and noise.

Evolution of Milan's Aspects

In a brainstorming session, Tellas had his Milan Screw Products employees list every aspect they could think of. "We make oil mist, steel turnings, heat. We heat oil, we heat machines, we make products," he states. "This was really rough, but we wanted to put everything down that we did. We then grouped the items into categories, such as oil mist and steel turnings that occur on the shop floor, and saturating absorbent masses and shop towels with oil that go outside the shop to be laundered. Other clusters included more esoteric items, such as throwing parts away, eating lunch, replacing copper air lines, grinding tools, and shredding paper." Tellas quips that they decided to continue eating lunch.

In addition to the list of aspects from all kinds of activities, Milan staff developed a list of purchased materials with potential substitutes and a comments column, and a second list of waste impacts, along with method of transport, destination, alternatives, and a comments column. In this way, every activity was addressed.

In Figure 6-2, we have provided examples of activities and their related environmental aspects, as well as the associated environmental impacts. One such example is an environmental aspect of aircraft maintenance (activity) that involves cleaning parts with solvents that emit vapors (aspect), causing air pollution (impact). Likewise, the spillage of fuels and lubricants and other environmental aspects of aircraft maintenance can result

One example of an activity is aircraft maintenance.

in soil and water pollution. Air, soil, and water pollution are environmental impacts caused by the activity of aircraft maintenance. ISO 14001 requires you identify all the aspects and impacts within your control.

FIGURE 6-2 Environmental Aspects and Related Impacts

Activity	Aspect	Impact
Aircraft maintenance	Use of cleaning solvents Spillage of fuels and lubricants	Air pollution Soil and water pollution
Construction	Earth moving Stormwater runoff	Soil erosion Water pollution
Reforestation	Habitat development	Erosion control Wildlife enhancement
Farming	Crop irrigation Herbicide application	Runoff erosion Water contamination
Drilling oil wells	Pipeline spills	Soil and water pollution

NOTE: Some of the impacts may be beneficial, such as the enhancement of wildlife that is a result of habitat development.

After identifying your organization's environmental aspects, you will need to determine which of these aspects can have significant impacts on the environment. Because the standard does not define "significant," you must make this distinction. Many organizations use a variety of methods to determine significance, such as numerical scoring or alphabetical ranking. We recommend that you also consider the severity and frequency of the impacts as indicators of significance.

Because working conditions can vary, the severity and frequency of an impact should be evaluated for normal and abnormal operating conditions. For example, routine maintenance is a normal operating condition, while an emergency shutdown constitutes an abnormal operating condition. An example of an aspects analysis is shown in Figure 6-3.

FIGURE 6-3 Determination of Significant Aspects

Activity	Aspects	Impacts	Legal	Community	Cost	Frequency	Corporate	Total Score	Significant >30
Operation: solid waste recycling									
Collect/sort recyclables	Energy use	Depletion of NR	1	1	2	1	1	6	—
Collect/sort recyclables	Decreased use of NR	Decreased landfill capacity	1	1	2	1	1	6	—
Collect/sort recyclables	Decreased use of NR	Decreased air emissions	1	1	2	1	1	6	—
Equipment use/maintenance	Energy use	Depletion of NR	1	1	2	1	1	6	—
Equipment use/maintenance (A)	Oil and grease spill	Air emission	3	1	2	1	1	8	—
Equipment use/maintenance (A)	Spills (HZ cleanup material)	Incineration (air)	5	1	2	1	20	29	—
Operation: utilities									
Utility operations	Energy use	Depletion of NR	1	1	1	5	1	9	—
Utility operations	Boilers - VOC emission	Air emission	5	1	1	5	1	13	—
Utility operations	Water vapors	Air emission	1	1	2	5	1	10	—
Utility operations	Chillers (CFC spill)	Air emission	5	1	1	5	20	32	X
Maintenance: HAZMAT disposal	Hazardous waste	Incineration (air)	5	1	2	3	20	31	—
Maintenance: HAZMAT disposal	Recycle	Decreased landfill capacity	3	1	3	5	1	13	—
Equipment maintenance	Spill	Air emission	5	1	1	5	20	32	X
Catastrophe (A)	Spill (fuel)	Increase to storm drain	5	1	2	1	20	29	—
Catastrophe (A)	Spill (CFC)	Air emission	5	1	1	1	20	28	—
Catastrophe (A)	Solid hazardous waste	Landfill capacity	3	1	2	1	1	8	—
Operation: bulk chemical and fuel storage									
Bulk storage	Spills (storm water)	Increase to storm drain	5	1	1	1	20	28	—
Bulk storage	Spills (air)	Air emissions	5	5	1	1	20	32	X
Bulk storage	Spills (ground)	Soil contamination	5	1	1	1	20	8	—
Bulk storage	Spills (HZ cleanup material)	Incineration (air)	5	1	1	1	20	8	—
Catastrophe (A)	Spills (storm water)	Increase to storm drain	5	5	1	1	20	32	—
Catastrophe (A)	Spills (air)	Air emissions	5	1	1	1	20	28	—
Catastrophe (A)	Spills (ground)	Soil contamination	5	1	1	1	20	28	—
Catastrophe (A)	Spills (HZ cleanup material)	Incineration (air)	5	1	1	1	20	28	—
Recharging batteries (N&A)	Spills (air)	Air emissions	5	1	2	2	20	30	—
Recharging batteries (N&A)	Spills (ground)	Soil contamination	5	1	1	1	20	28	—
Recharging batteries (N&A)	Spills (HZ cleanup material)	Incineration (air)	5	1	1	1	20	28	—

Make sure to document the planning process to show how significant aspects were identified. This documentation will be useful during third-party audits and when the evaluation is updated.

It is a requirement of ISO 14001 to keep environmental aspect and impact information up to date. We suggest an annual review of aspects and impacts. Environmental aspects and impacts should also be reevaluated when major operational changes take place.

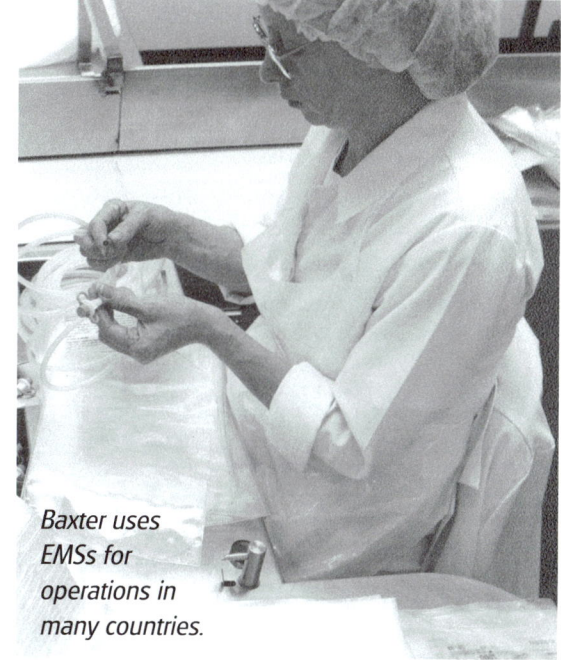

Baxter uses EMSs for operations in many countries.

One company held a one-day workshop on understanding the ISO 14001 standard, ending the day with a brainstorming session to sort out aspects and impacts. They realized that everything that comes into the plant as a raw material leaves as a product, waste, or recyclable material. They sorted aspects and impacts into six categories:

1. Water use and discharge.

2. Air emissions.

3. Solid waste (including hazardous waste).

4. Resource and energy.

5. Chemical.

6. Nuisance—noise and odor that are not ecological issues but are annoying.

All items were then ranked against five different kinds of impacts. The impacts were regulatory (fines), community (anything offsite, such as fire department, neighbors), customer (ability to be a good supplier), employees (safety concerns), and business (cost). Each item was scored on scale of +3 to –3 against each impact.

The aspects team decided that a +3, an opportunity, needed to be on the significant aspects list to continue to improve and that a –3 was a risk to try to mitigate. If the item was neutral (0), it didn't make the significant aspects list. The research and ratings were performed by the aspects team, who then reported back to the EMS steering team. The aspects team was made up of employees drawn from major company departments.

However you elect to score and identify your significant aspects, be aware that the operations associated with your significant aspects have to have documented controls (procedures) around them (see 4.4.6). For this reason, ensure that you are identifying the significant aspects—which are typically 10 to 15 percent of the total—of your operations. Otherwise, you may find yourself generating many new procedures.

4.3.2 Legal and Other Requirements

Central to the successful operation of an EMS is the identification of legal and other requirements. The standard requires that a procedure be in place to do this. Legal requirements include relevant local, state, and federal regulations that apply to your operations. For example, what discharge permits (air, water) are you required to have? How do you track these?

The environmental affairs department (which may be a group or an individual) in some organizations has several means of identifying applicable rules and regulations, ranging from subscriptions to regulatory update services to retained legal counsel.

The "other" category could include (a) being a member of Responsible Care, (b) a purchase agreement that requires cleanup of a contaminated site, or (c) an agreement comparable to the one between McDonalds and the Environmental Defense Fund that restricts McDonalds' use of styrofoam containers. It is important that the organization identify, categorize, and understand legal and other requirements that apply to its activities.

4.3.3 Objectives and Targets

Once significant environmental aspects have been identified and legal and other obligations have been determined, the organization must develop environmental objectives and targets. ISO 14001 defines these as follows:

An EMS applies to any kind of industry or organization.

"Environmental objective: overall goal, arising from the environmental policy that an organization sets itself to achieve, and which is quantified wherever practical."

"Environmental target: detailed performance requirements, quantified wherever practicable, applicable to the organization or parts thereof, that arise from the environmental objectives and that need to be set and met in order to achieve those objectives."

In developing objectives and targets that can apply across the organization or to specific activities, the employees who will be responsible for achieving the objectives and targets should be involved with setting them.

Establishing Objectives and Targets

In many organizations, senior management sets high-level environmental objectives for the entire organization. After these are established, each department or division is responsible for developing department-specific environmental targets to meet these objectives. Environmental targets that support the objectives must be specific, measurable, and detailed. The identified objectives and targets are documented, as required by the standard.

Figure 6-4 lists examples of objectives and targets.

FIGURE 6-4 Objectives and Targets

Objectives	Targets
Reduce water consumption	Establish water use baseline by 7/1/03. Benchmark each facility by 10/1/03. Have a water reduction plan initiated by 1/1/2004.
Reduce spills	Complete a spill management workshop, $1^{st}Q03$. Reduce number of spills from 2002 by 10%.
Eliminate methylene chloride	Evaluate alternatives by 6/1/03. Evaluate new non-methylene chloride process by 6/1/03. Implement new process by 12/31/03.

Figure 6-5 shows how one company tracks progress against its targets for reduction in energy use monthly and annually. Note how this is tracked by unit of production—in this case silicon wafers. This method allows for fluctuations in production volumes.

It is important to note that you are **not** required to have an objective and/or target for every significant aspect. You **are** required to consider your significant aspects when setting your objectives and targets.

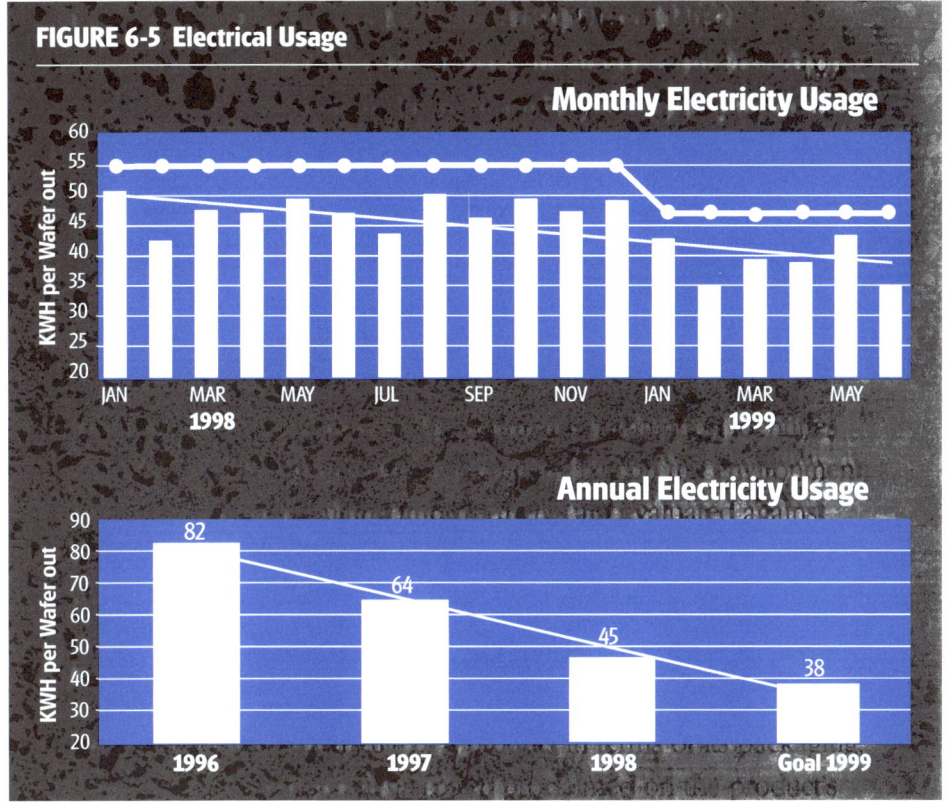

FIGURE 6-5 Electrical Usage

4.3.4 Environmental Management Program(s)

The final phase of EMS planning is to establish environmental management programs, which must identify precisely how each objective and target will be met, including assigned time frames and personnel. ISO 14001 requires that organizations establish mechanisms for EMS objectives and targets to be achieved. Responsibility and resources must be designated, with time frames set for meeting the objectives and targets within an environmental management program.

Most organizations use the annual budgeting process as a means to determine funding needs for the EMS. At this time, specific programs are identified that will support the objectives and targets for the new fiscal year. In addition, the company needs to provide resources to the departments and divisions so they are able to meet the demands of objectives and targets established by the EMS.

Some EMS Financial Wins

Many companies have realized substantial cost savings through implementation and use of their environmental management systems, and have tracked their financial successes. Here are a few examples, drawn from *http://www.bsi.com*:

Electrolux Home Products (formerly Frigidaire) in Greenville, Michigan avoided a $70,000 fine for a spill by a contractor because the company followed procedures for contractor work onsite as required by the Electrolux EMS.

Delphi Saginaw in Michigan identified an opportunity to reduce water treatment costs by 40 percent and cut energy costs by 20 percent ($2.5 million annually), by initiating "energy walks" during periodic shutdowns.

General Motors' Flint Metal Center in Michigan documented tremendous energy savings and increased revenue through better waste management. Energy savings alone paid for developing and implementing an EMS. ■

Notes 6

The Baxter environmental team at the I.V. Systems plant in Cartago, Costa Rica, helped win national recognition for the facility's conservation efforts.

Chapter 7
4.4 Implementation and Operation

The **implementation** and operation section of ISO 14001 is the *do* portion of the Plan-Do-Check-Act improvement loop.

The Standard Requires...

When planning is complete, implementation begins. Section 4.4 of ISO 14001 includes seven elements: structure and responsibility; training, awareness, and competence; communication; environmental management system documentation; document control; operational control; and emergency preparedness and response. Implementation is time-consuming and can be frustrating since you and your team are trying to alter behavior and habits. Your efforts will be rewarded when employees begin to be enthusiastic about the EMS and realize that the organization takes the environment seriously. As one EMS manager said when her EMS was implemented, "People have a lot more respect for what I do."

4.4.1 Structure and Responsibility

This element of the standard is very clear. The organization must:

- Define EMS management responsibility and authority.
- Provide resources for the EMS.
- Appoint one or more people to be responsible for the EMS.

The appointment of a specific management representative is required by ISO 14001. In addition to performing his or her regular responsibilities, the representative must ensure that the EMS is maintained and implemented. This person (or people), appointed by top management, is also responsible for reporting on EMS performance, and has the authority to ensure that necessary training takes place, corrective action reports are filed, corrections are made, and documentation is developed and kept up to date.

Clearly defined roles and responsibilities for operating the EMS come from a management structure that should be established early in the implementation process to provide people with the authority to implement the EMS. Senior managers need to send a clear message to employees that the EMS is an integral part of operations.

Many companies have found that structure and responsibilities can be addressed by establishing an EMS steering committee that has a senior management sponsor. This group is responsible for getting the EMS up and running. Once the system is established, members of the steering committee may have ongoing EMS responsibilities.

The steering committee should have a layered, cross-functional structure with defined EMS responsibilities. The environmental manager is often designated by top management to ensure that the EMS is implemented and to report on its performance.

Personnel whose jobs may impact the environment should have clearly written job descriptions so they understand the importance of certain job duties.

action items

Structure

- Create an organization chart.
- Use a responsibilities matrix.
- Let people know the goals of your team.
- Build team pride by setting and meeting goals.
- Have an EMS team charter.
- Have job responsibilities outlined in your EMS manual. See 4.4.4.

4.4.2 Training, Awareness, and Competence

Many organizations have environmental training programs in place to cover the regulatory requirements of their businesses, such as hazardous waste handling, spill response training, and HAZWOPER.

This element of ISO 14001 expresses a clear expectation for training and awareness. Training applies to personnel whose jobs could have a significant impact on the environment, such as emergency response teams, wastewater plant operators, and environmental technicians. Awareness applies to all employees.

action items

Training

- Develop a written training plan that addresses new employees, annual refresher training, and specialized training.

- Structure the training by topics and levels, such as environmental awareness (all employees) vs. environmental compliance (some employees).

- Use a variety of training techniques to get your message across. Adult learners respond well to visual, hands-on training.

- Use a variety of media to reinforce your message, such as posters, brown bags, videos, overheads, and quizzes.

- Don't forget to use color and humor.

ISO 14001 requires that *"all personnel whose work may create a significant impact upon the environment receive appropriate training."* Personnel must be competent on the basis of appropriate training and education if they perform tasks that can cause significant impacts on the environment. EMS training can be integrated into existing programs or provided separately.

7

Drawing Contractors into the EMS

Laura Fiffick tells contractors about the EMS and has them sign the environmental policy, requiring them to adhere to the Port of Houston's goals. She says that this process could become more formalized when they get into the EMS with engineering, and has thought about developing a video about the significance of the EMS that explains what contractors need to do. An ISO 14001 training video worked well for employees. (Shaw Environmental customized a video for the Port Authority, filming the executive director as if he is talking to the employees, about why the EMS is important.)

EMS awareness programs are directed at employees at all levels and functions, and must include, at a minimum, an awareness of the environmental policy and the basic goals of the EMS. Because the planning process singles out activities associated with significant aspects and impacts, managers must determine who needs to be properly trained, qualified, and made aware of the EMS.

Creative Employee Awareness at Baxter

Ricardo Valverde, EHS Manager for Corporate Facilities in Illinois, explains that the EMS awareness program at Baxter International's Costa Rica facility consisted of contests, small gifts for filling out surveys, posters, buttons, and crossword puzzles with ISO 14001 terminology. They had videos and speakers at lunchtime with flyers, bombarding employees with information about ISO. Artistic employees submitted logo designs in a logo design contest for the ISO 14001 awareness program.

"After six months of a political campaign—which is what it amounted to," Valverde quips, "employees had a good sense of the program, even though many did not attend secondary schools. One of the questions employees were asked was for the best definition of an aspect. They marked their answers on a form provided and put them in a box in the cafeteria. We chose three winners who received cash prizes, but we also had tee shirts with logos, which every employee received. We then publicized the winners' names and posted the correct answers on the bulletin board."

Although ISO 14001 does not require contractors to be trained as part of the EMS, the EMS implementation team needs to decide whether this should be done. Contractor duties could significantly impact the environment, which would mean that they must meet the same EMS requirements as company employees.

BP Exploration recognized this need as they had an estimated 1,500 contractor personnel supporting 1,200 BP employees in exploring and producing oil on Alaska's North Slope. Norman Ingram, who is manager of compliance assurance and continual improvement for BP, acted as EMS implementation manager.

Try an EMS Training Video

BP Exploration Alaska, Inc. made quite an investment in training for the EMS. "We took a multi-level approach," Ingram observes, "preparing a 10-minute video that can be viewed with a VCR or individually at a work station through the intranet. This allows anyone in the BP world to look at this. We also provided classes that were three to four hours in duration, going through a fairly crisp explanation of each of the sub-elements of the standard and how our program relates to these."

"For the work force in general, we set up toolbox meetings, running the video tape followed by a discussion of how the objectives and targets had been set and how their work relates to each of these. This process made the EMS much more real to the employees." At all North Slope BP sites, Ingram points out, there is a weekly meeting of 45 minutes to an hour on safety and environmental issues, plus employees take a few minutes daily to discuss safety, health, and environmental issues. He states that these practices are integral to the BP culture.

Maintaining training records is a critical part of the EMS. You need to know which employees have received training, as well as updates on new training requirements and procedures. These records should be maintained according to your records retention procedure, element 4.5.3.

Evaluate the effectiveness of your EMS training and awareness program by asking for feedback from employees. Employees can expect to be interviewed on their EMS training during an EMS audit. Make the training interesting and keep the message simple and direct. This helps employees retain and more easily retrieve relevant information when responding during an audit.

4.4.3 Communication

The standard requires procedures for internal and external communications, both of which are essential for a successful EMS. This can be challenging, as environmental issues have historically been addressed by a specialist or group within the organization. Unlike more typical one-way organizational communication, EMS communications seek out employee input and feedback.

Internal Communication

Internal communications are required to keep employees informed about the EMS, environmental aspects and impacts, and regulatory requirements. Organizations can add EMS issues to the routine internal communications, such as management and safety meetings, e-mail, newsletters, staff meetings, and bulletin boards. These are some of the best ways to communicate internally.

> **Getting Through to Employees**
>
> *Paul Steucke of Ft. Lewis states that the most difficult internal communication hurdle was changing the culture of the organization and overcoming the general inertia. "You're going to get resistance because you are changing the way they do their jobs," he noted. "The first thing they saw was a lot of added work and rewrites of standard operating procedures. I knew we had turned the corner when I started hearing them using the new lingo, talking about P/CARs, the web-based preventive and corrective action reports. It also helped that public works is essentially an engineering organization, so the engineers naturally gravitated toward a systems approach."*

External Communication

The standard requires an external communication procedure that addresses receiving, documenting, and responding to outside inquiries. This requirement is met in many organizations by identifying a single point-of-contact for all external environmental information and communication requests.

Figure 7-1 is an example of an external environmental communication procedure.

FIGURE 7-1 External Environmental Communication Procedures Form

HANDLING A TELEPHONE CALL INQUIRY

Thank the caller for calling, and state that someone who has the needed information will return the call in 20 to 30 minutes. Ask for the caller's name, company, and telephone number.

Note: Do not make any comments concerning incidents or potential incidents, or give out any other information, such as names or phone numbers. Document:

Date _____ Time _____
Caller's Name _____ Caller's Telephone Number ( ) _____
Reason for Call: _____
_____
_____

FORWARDING INFORMATION FROM THE CALLER

Initial Call (8 to 5, Monday through Friday)   Human Resources Secretary
Alternate Contact (8 to 5, Monday through Friday)   Safety and Environmental
Evening/Weekends: Contact Security at _____
Security will contact HR from the confidential home phone list.
Forwarded to _____ By _____

FOLLOW-UP WITH CALLER

Called Back _____ Date _____ Time _____
Nature of the Call _____
_____

Resolution _____
_____
_____

Comments _____
Staff Name _____ Job Title _____ Dept. _____

ISO 14001 requires that the point-of-contact:

- Identify the most qualified employee to respond to the inquiry, and route the inquiry to that person.
- Maintain records of inquiries and responses.
- Ensure that all inquiries receive a response in a timely manner.

In addition to a procedure for external communication, ISO 14001 requires that the *"organization shall consider processes for external communication on its significant environmental aspects and record its decision."* What this means is that a discussion is held on how much of the EMS is made public. ISO 14001 requires that only the environmental policy be made public. Many companies that have an ISO 14001 EMS publish annual environmental reports on their progress in meeting objectives and targets.

The EMS team and management must decide the type and level of environmental information it will make public. Web pages on a company internet site are often the location of choice for annual environmental reports or data about significant environmental aspects, and the results of organizational programs to reduce or mitigate associated impacts. If the organization decides not to provide external communication on its significant environmental aspects, this decision must be recorded.

Baxter International releases its external communications annually in the form of the *Baxter Sustainability Report*, a publication of more than 50 pages that is available on request or can be read on the company's website at *http://www.baxter.com/ehs*. The report covers the economic, social, and environmental aspects of sustainability of the company worldwide.

The Port of Houston Authority's Communications

"The Port of Houston has an expansion project going on that is not well liked by some businesses in the community," Laura Fiffick explains. "I realized that we did a lot of good things environmentally but that we never told anyone about them. I thought that an EMS would be a way to document and verify that we have a good system. Our compliance program was good but it was command and control. The ISO 14001 EMS let us go to the employees and show them how their actions can impact the bay, the same bay that they want to be clean for fishing. We asked them what they could do to reduce their impacts on the bay. We have had unbelievable innovations from our employees because they really took hold of the program; they became the motivators."

And has the certification to ISO 14001 been useful in reassuring the community about the expansion project? The answer is a resounding yes. When the project manager told the community that the port had two facilities that were certified, one person quipped, "Well, that's all fine, but Bayport will never be certified." The project manager quickly responded, "Actually, we are committed to ISO 14001 certification in our permit to the Army Corp of Engineers." The complaints stopped immediately.

4.4.4. Environmental Management System Documentation

This element of the standard addresses how you should compile and maintain information that describes core elements of your EMS and their interaction, and how directions to related documentation are addressed.

Many organizations develop an EMS manual or index, comparable to the manual in a quality management system. As shown in Figure 7-2, the EMS manual is a high-level document (Level 1) that summarizes the management system and refers to more detailed documents and procedures of the EMS. This manual provides

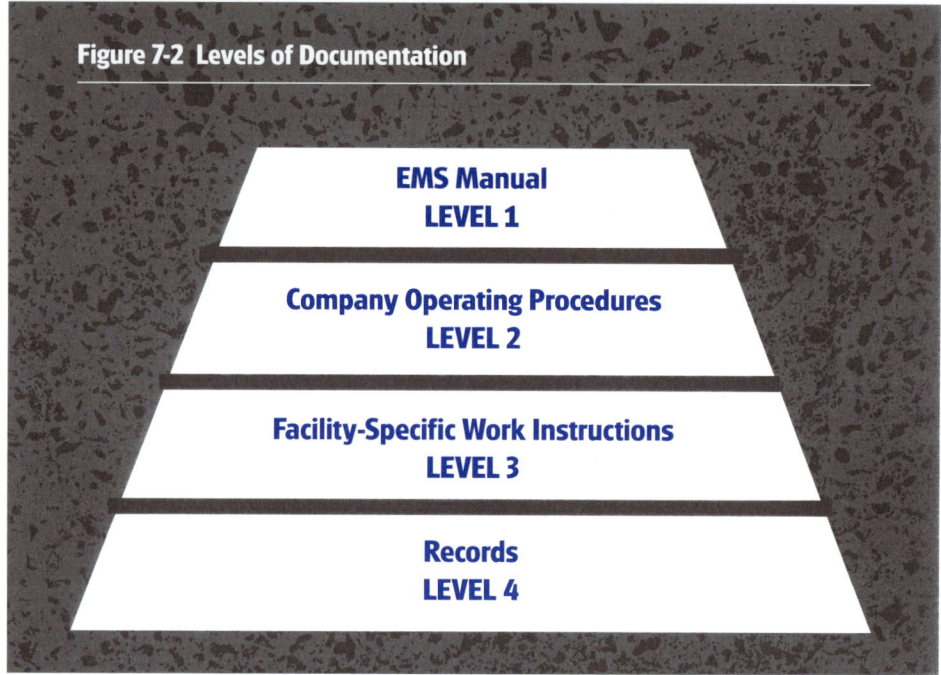

Figure 7-2 Levels of Documentation

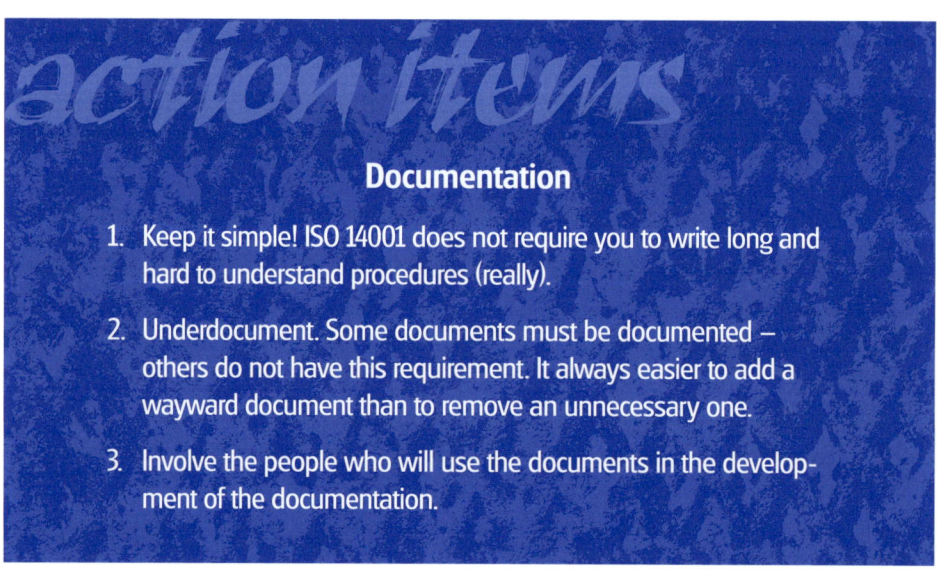

Documentation

1. Keep it simple! ISO 14001 does not require you to write long and hard to understand procedures (really).

2. Underdocument. Some documents must be documented – others do not have this requirement. It always easier to add a wayward document than to remove an unnecessary one.

3. Involve the people who will use the documents in the development of the documentation.

links to specific procedures (Level 2) and work instructions (Level 3) that are part of the EMS.

This manual can be used as a tool by employees and auditors to find their way around the EMS, and as a means to find information on specific EMS responsibilities. The EMS manual can be developed either on paper or in electronic form. Several companies have found that the EMS manual can most easily be accessed through an intranet system.

BP's Intranet EMS

BP's EMS is on an intranet system, with microwave and fiberoptic cable for offshore rigs. The company is strongly oriented toward making good use of technology, so documents can be called up in Azerbaijan or Western Australia as easily as they can in Alaska. Ingram states that this allows the advantage of sharing knowledge; a new group can tap into needed information quickly and easily.

English is BP's predominant business language, but in Colombia and other parts of the world, the EMS is in multiple languages. Much of the EMS can be accessed in eight to ten languages in the more than 100 countries where BP has facilities.

An intranet EMS is easy to access and update.

After core elements of the EMS are defined and documented, the system elements can be summarized in your manual. A recommended approach is to organize the manual using the same format as the ISO 14001 standard. Each element of the standard should be addressed. The EMS manual should be integrated with existing procedures, work instructions, and documents.

4.4.5 Document Control

ISO 14001 requires that the organization establish and maintain a system for controlling all EMS documentation. To be effective, such a document control system should provide a standard format for documents, and their approval, distribution, review, and removal of outdated documents.

People are often confused about the distinctions between documents and records. A **document** describes how a part of the EMS operates—what happens, how to do it. A **record** provides evidence that an action has been performed.

For example, a procedure that describes how aspects are determined is a **document**. The complete list of the aspects is a **record**. A spill response plan is an EMS **document**; a spill cleanup training log is an EMS **record**. A pH monitoring procedure is an EMS **document**; effluent discharge pH readings are EMS **records**.

This element of ISO 14001 is meant to ensure that employees have current, accurate, authentic, and complete information upon which to make decisions. This information is controlled, not to restrict access, but to limit the inadvertent use of faulty data. Organizations with ISO 9001:2000 systems in place can incorporate the EMS document control requirements very easily into their existing document control systems. The following is a suggested process for establishing a document control system if you do not already have one.

Document Control System Tips

1. **Determine EMS Document Control Needs.**

   Review existing document control processes, and interview potential users of the document control system to determine what type of system would be most effective. For example, identify the types of information that need to be controlled, how these will be distributed, and who needs access to the information.

2. **Define Templates for EMS Documents.**

   Design a template to be used to house EMS data and information.

3. **Establish EMS Document Control Procedures.**

   Document defining procedures for creating new EMS documents, defining who creates the document, who reviews and approves the document, and how the document is distributed and users are trained.

4. **Implement the EMS Document Control System.**

   Install and operate the document control system. You will need a plan for converting existing data, information, and documents, as needed, into the new formats.

Let the Documentation Suit Your Organization

Allan Ricketts of Trus Joist says that they don't have an online system. In several smaller manufacturing plants, employees use a variety of hand tools and drill presses to manufacture trusses. These plants do not have electronic workstations on the plant floor. Other larger plants, such as the Kenora plant in Ontario that has large presses and de-barkers, do have workstations. The company uses a manual system printed on color-coded paper to denote control documents with specific formats and headers.

"We have a business systems manual, a best operating practices manual, and job instructions, as well as approved documents and forms," Ricketts explains. "The EMS manuals are in information centers on the plant floor so they are available to all associates. Designated employees are responsible for adding updated pages to the manuals. As we build Kenora up, we will still have the paper copies but we will migrate those documents to an online system, and you would view them at a workstation electronically."

Similarly, Milan Screw Products has one paper EMS manual that is in the office in the center of the plant. With only 22 employees operating heavy metal cutting machinery at one plant, multiple workstations are neither necessary nor practical.

4.4.6 Operational Control

Operations and activities that are associated with your significant environmental aspects are addressed in this element of ISO 14001.

The standard requires that these operations and activities be identified and planned *"to ensure they are carried out under specified conditions."* In addition, as stated in the standard, the organization must establish and maintain *"procedures related to the significant environmental aspects of goods and services used by the organization, and communicating relevant procedures and requirements to suppliers and contractors."*

Work instructions and manuals can be used to guide critical work activities, establishing guidance and procedures for critical functions related to a broad range of duties. These can provide strong control of processes and activities. There are three steps involved in developing operational controls:

Review Operations and Activities

Identify the operations and activities that are associated with your significant environmental aspects to determine whether they are carried out under specified conditions. Specified conditions also include documented procedures *"to cover situations where their absence could lead to deviations from the environmental policy and the objectives and targets."*

Develop Operational Controls

Develop or revise operational controls associated with significant environmental aspects, and appropriate work control measures and systems using people familiar with these activities. Written procedures are a common method for controlling operations. The qualifications and skills of the employees who will be performing the activity should be taken into account when deciding who develops the procedures. When possible, written environmental procedures should be incorporated into existing documentation, such as standard operating procedures.

Review Activities of Suppliers and Contractors

Working with contractors and suppliers is a critical component of operational control. It is necessary to determine which goods and services are directly tied to identified significant aspects. Once you know which suppliers can impact your environmental performance, you will need to communicate relevant procedures and requirements to those suppliers and contractors.

ISO 14001 does not require ISO 14001 certification of contractors and suppliers, although this has become a customer requirement in some industries.

> ### Baxter's Contractor Programs in Costa Rica and China
>
> *Valverde says that his site has about ten contractors, most of whom work onsite. "All of them have to go through at least an annual general meeting for all contractors that lasts a day," he explains. "We bring up all the policies and practices of Baxter, and explain ISO 14001, as most of the contractors want to know about the standard. In fact, the contractors, health ministry, and the environmental ministry send personnel to visit our facility to see what an ISO 14001-certified facility looks like."*
>
> *Any contractor coming onto the Baxter site in Costa Rica must also receive specific one-on-one training for EHS and Baxter practices. Valverde offers the example of a welder who has been through the annual training, but still has to go through a one-hour training session on environmental health and safety before he can work onsite. The welder then has to sign a form acknowledging Baxter's rules, and must sign a training roster to demonstrate that he has been through the training program.*

4.4.7 Emergency Preparedness and Response

This element of the standard requires the organization to have established procedures to identify potential emergency situations, to respond to emergencies, and to mitigate any resulting environmental impacts. After accidents or emergencies occur, the emergency preparedness and response procedures must be reviewed for effectiveness. The organization must test response procedures where practical.

Many organizations in North America are well prepared to satisfy this requirement, as the law requires that operations involved in the storage, use, and treatment of fuels and chemicals have emergency spill and response plans in place.

EMS improvements can be made in the documentation for identifying potential accidents and increasing the level of awareness of personnel who have specific roles and responsibilities. In many organizations, this is accomplished by routine training. The following steps are recommended to review your organization's status under this element of ISO 14001. ■

Emergency Preparedness and Response Tips

1. **Review Hazards.**

   Identify operations and activities where an emergency could cause a significant environmental impact. Complete an assessment of hazards and associated emergency preparedness and response actions. Revise and update emergency preparedness and response procedures as necessary.

2. **Review Existing Documentation.**

   Review existing plans, procedures, and supporting documentation for emergency preparedness and response. Review the emergency preparedness and response program.

3. **Review Awareness of Emergency Response Procedures.**

   Ensure that emergency plans and procedures have been well communicated both internally and externally. Employees need to know about the potential emergencies that could occur and the appropriate responses to be taken.

4. **Review Revision and Testing Requirements.**

   Review the revision and testing requirements of the emergency response system to ensure that both processes are appropriately documented.

Notes

BP monitors its operations at the Manifold building on the North Slope of Alaska.

Chapter 8
4.5 Checking and Corrective Action

Environmental objectives and targets are established during the EMS planning phase. Meeting these goals is accomplished by implementing training and awareness programs and ensuring widespread communication and documented procedures for critical operations. The checking and corrective action element of the standard, which is the ***check*** portion of the improvement loop, allows you to measure how well your EMS is working.

The Standard Requires...

Element 4.5 of ISO 14001 addresses how to:

- Monitor and measure the EMS.
- Respond to nonconformances.
- Implement corrective and preventive actions.
- Maintain environmental records.
- Establish an EMS audit program.

4.5.1 Monitoring and Measurement

Monitoring and measurement consists of ongoing data collection and continual tracking of specified parameters. An ISO 14001 monitoring and measurement system should include:

- Documented procedures to regularly monitor and measure the key characteristics of your operations and activities that can have significant environmental impacts.
- Methods to record data that tracks performance, relevant operational controls, and conformance with environmental objectives and targets.
- Procedures used to calibrate monitoring equipment and keep calibration records.
- A documented procedure for periodically evaluating compliance with environmental regulations.

Monitoring and Measurement

Organizations monitor their operations to comply with environmental regulations, to determine the effectiveness of ongoing operations, to assess the consequences of accidents, and to provide public assurance. Because monitoring may already be ongoing, many existing monitoring activities may be in conformance with the standard.

Full conformance to ISO 14001 monitoring and measurement will be achieved when actual performance is measured against objectives and targets.

After key characteristics for monitoring are identified, monitoring and measurement protocols need to be established. We recommend that you incorporate EMS monitoring protocols into existing monitoring activities to avoid redundancy.

Tracking Progress at BP

BP used direct metrics and detailed action tracking systems for preventive and corrective actions to follow items to closure. Norman Ingram says they also closely track compliance to laws, regulations, and over 800 active permits associated with their operations. Progress is monitored on a daily, weekly, or monthly basis, as well as quarterly and annually. Ingram says they also analyze trends. Performance is evaluated from management on down through the company, greatly aided by the online system. There is also a corporate compliance committee that looks closely at EMS performance.

Calibration Procedures

ISO 14001 requires that monitoring equipment be calibrated and calibration records be maintained. For example, if the pH of wastewater effluent is a key indicator, then the pH meter will need to be calibrated to ensure accurate readings are being recorded. You will need to establish and document procedures for ensuring that all monitoring equipment is calibrated and that calibration records are maintained.

Compliance Evaluation

As part of 4.5.1, a routine compliance check must be performed. This can be done through formal compliance audits performed in-house or by a third party. ISO 14001 does not specify a compliance audit but requires that the organization establish and maintain *"a documented procedure for periodically evaluating compliance with relevant environmental legislation and regulations."* Many organizations cover this requirement by conducting annual compliance audits.

However, this requirement could also be satisfied by, for example, a daily inspection of effluent discharge records to ensure they are meeting permitted levels and routine inspections of hazardous waste storage areas to make certain that storage times are not being exceeded. If you decide to use inspections instead of audits to evaluate your compliance, make sure the inspections address *all* of your compliance obligations.

> ### EMS and Compliance Issues at BP
>
> "Many companies have found that they could have an EMS that met ISO 14001 standards, and could be setting objectives and targets, and meeting or exceeding these in areas, such as pollution prevention, but could still have compliance issues," Norman Ingram states. "We learned some hard but valuable lessons from a situation in 1995 involving one of our contractors mishandling some hazardous waste. We found out about it from a whistle-blower. Following an extensive government investigation, the contractor, and subsequently BP, deemed to have ultimate responsibility as operator of the oilfield, entered into plea agreements." The contractor and BP were put on probation for five years.
>
> One of Ingram's main responsibilities is to oversee the requirements that came out of that case. As a result of this issue, the contractor now has a superior EMS in place and BP has significantly revamped its EMS to enhance the focus and specificity around compliance. BP also requires all its contractors to have and maintain a compliance-focused EMS when work involves environmental issues.

4.5.2 Nonconformance and Corrective and Preventive Action

ISO 14001 requires that an organization establish, maintain, and use a system to identify conformance and nonconformances with the EMS, and to have a system for handling, investigating, and correcting nonconformances. The standard also requires that organizations be proactive and keep records of preventive measures taken to avoid nonconformances.

Note: Nonconformance refers to deviations from EMS requirements and should not be confused with noncompliance. The term noncompliance refers to deviations from federal, state, and local environmental regulations.

Responsibilities and authorities for taking action must be defined in the system. A good corrective and preventive action system should focus on issues that have the largest risk and impact on the organization, and then on ensuring that the same issues are permanently corrected so they do not recur.

The purpose of this element of the standard is to ensure that oversight and management of the EMS is achieved and a mechanism is in place that allows corrections and improvements to be made. While it is very important to have a good corrective action process in place, organizations are expected to be more proactive than reactive. The preventive action side of the system should be equally as strong as or stronger than the corrective action side.

Corrective Actions at Baxter

Mike Cycyota, Director of the Corporate EHS Audit Program for Baxter International, states that all systems audits performed in the company require action plans, which include listing the persons responsible for closure, the anticipated timeline, and the corrective actions to be taken to address both immediate issues and underlying causes. One division came up with a web-based nonconformance log. By working with the corporate group, this system was expanded companywide with the nonconformances made accessible through the EHS home page of the Baxter intranet system.

"In this way," he states, "everyone can utilize it but it is password-protected. Any nonconformity will be listed, whether a compliance issue or ISO 14001, and will likewise come from a variety of sources, such as self-identified, spotted during a routine walk-through, or an item from a formal audit." He adds that individual sites could limit access, but that division managers would have access to all of the division information, and corporate managers would have access to everything.

Developing a Nonconformance Procedure

The following steps will help you establish a nonconformance procedure:

Identify Systems for Handling EMS Nonconformances

The system must be accessible to all parts of the organization and must:

- Define responsibility and authority for handling and investigating nonconformances.
- Initiate and perform corrective and preventive actions.
- Implement and record changes to documented EMS procedures that result from corrective or preventive actions.

We suggest that you use a form to document identified nonconformances to specify authority for employees who can identify a nonconformance, as well as carefully defined processes for performing the analysis and actions required. Many companies use a continual improvement form (CIF) that addresses these needs. See the Trus Joist example on pages 94-95.

Implement Nonconformance and Corrective and Preventive Action

As with other EMS components, the system must be implemented throughout the organization. When this system is new, make sure that issues are reported and that appropriate corrective and preventive actions are taken in a timely manner.

Integrate with Existing Programs and Activities

The EMS corrective and preventive action system can be integrated with existing corrective action systems. Companies that are certified to ISO 9001:2000 can easily adapt their quality management corrective action system to include the EMS, perhaps combining their quality and environmental audits as well (4.5.4).

Trus Joist Continual Improvement Form (CIF)

CONTINUAL IMPROVEMENT FORM (CIF)

Indicate if – SMS, QMS, or EMS	SMS	QMS	EMS	CIF #
Circle Appropriate Category	1 – Internal Audit, 2 – External Audit, 3 – Cust. Complaint/Field Problem, 4 – Associate Suggestion, 5 – Nonconforming Product, 6 – Supplier Problem, 7 – Document Change Request, 8 – Preventive Action, 9 – Corrective Action, 10 – Air Quality, 11 – Storm Water, 12 – Other			

Originator Completes Section "A" and forwards to their Supervisor, Auditor, MR (or designees).

A. Originator's Name: Date: Return Completed Copy?   Y or N

Reference: (BOP #, JI #, SMS #, Element #, Form, Part #, P.O. #, Job # as appropriate)

Responsible Dept. or Indiv.

Description of Condition

Immediate Action Taken (if any)

Originator's Supervisor, Auditee, MR or their designees Approve Section "B" and forwards to MR (or designee).

B. CIF Approved By:	Date:	
MR (or designee) completes Sect. "C", initials and forwards to the Assigned Individual		MR Initials:
C. Assigned to:	Target Response Date:	

Responsible Department, Team, or Individual Completes Section "D" by analyzing why Section "A" occurred.

D. Root Cause:

1. Why did the condition in Section A occur?

2. Why did the condition in #1 occur:

3. Why did the condition in #2 occur?

4. Why did the condition in #3 occur?

TJ ™ Deerwood Plant   Revision: 10   Effective Date: 8/2/02

CONTINUAL IMPROVEMENT FORM (CIF) (Pg. 2)

Upon completion of Root Cause Analysis, the Responsible Department, Team, or Individual completes Section "E." Approval of Section "E" is evident from the "Assigned To" individual's signature. The CIF is then returned to the MR (or designee).

NOTE: If the Preventive and/or Corrective Action cannot be completed by the Target Response Date, Fill-in the Target Completion Date and forward to MR (or designee) for approval.

E. Preventive and/or Corrective Action Taken:	Target Completion Date:	MR Approval:

Request further review of this CIF with Management Team	YES	NO	If Yes, Date Reviewed:

Signature: Date:

If the Preventive and/or Corrective Action involves review of procedures by Associates, use this area to identify exactly what was reviewed and obtain signatures of those reviewing this information.

Follow-up of Preventive and/or Corrective Action is conducted by Originator, Internal Auditor, MR, DMR (or designees).

F. Follow-Up Signature: Date:

Follow-Up Details (was the Preventive and/or Corrective Action effective?):

MR or designee completes Section "G" upon completion of Section "F."

G. Close-Out Signature: (signature indicates successful completion of CIF and is proof of review.)   Date:

TJ™ Deerwood Plant   Revision: 10   Effective Date: 8/2/02

4.5.3 Records

Maintaining and using environmental records is an important part of a well-designed EMS. An organization can demonstrate conformance with ISO 14001 requirements through its environmental records and can track progress toward meeting established objectives and targets. Records must be readily available, and maintained and protected from damage, deterioration, or loss.

You will need to identify your environmental records. At a minimum, the environmental records must include training records, audit results, and management review records. Some examples of other environmental records include:

- Documented significant aspects.
- Documented objectives and targets.
- Corrective action reports.
- Training records.
- Internal audit records.
- Management reviews.
- Internal communication records.
- External communication records.
- Records of third-party audits.
- Calibration records.

It is important to track environmental records carefully.

Document and define record keeping practices to be used for all EMS records in a records procedure. In this procedure, methods must be defined for identifying, collecting, indexing, accessing, filing, storing, maintaining, and disposing of EMS records.

All employees who have defined responsibilities for collecting EMS records must be trained in these practices and understand what is expected of them.

4.5.4 Environmental Management System Audit

ISO 14001 (3.6) defines an environmental management system audit as *"a systematic and documented verification process of objectively obtaining and evaluating evidence to determine whether an organization's environmental management system conforms to the environmental management system audit criteria set by the organization..."* The standard also requires that these results be communicated to management.

Internal and external audits are conducted to determine whether your EMS conforms to ISO 14001 and is being implemented and maintained. The audits also provide informational feedback to management.

An effective audit program has these characteristics:

- Audits are conducted on a published schedule.
- Trained, independent auditors perform the audits.
- Audit results are documented.
- Managers of the audited departments correct nonconformances in their areas.

ISO 14001 does not require you to have an internal audit program. However, you cannot solely rely on the external, third party auditors to verify that your EMS is functioning, as they will not provide you with enough feedback. It is strongly recommended that you develop an internal audit program.

Your very first internal audit should be a baseline audit of your current system to identify gaps between your system and the standard. Your implementation will then be focused on closing the gaps.

Auditing Incentives at Trus Joist

Allan Ricketts of Trus Joist explains that his company wants people fully engaged in the process when auditing the EMS, recognizing that they must learn new skills and apply their judgment in an effective way. For these reasons, the company has a number of incentives for auditors—these vary from plant to plant—ranging from extra money per hour for audits to specific pay for the audit, or awards of jackets or dining out on the company. He notes that these incentives set a standard that employees strive to meet, resulting in very good internal audits.

Every plant has from seven to twenty trained internal auditors who conduct audits monthly for safety, quality, environmental, and sustainable forestry. Ricketts states, "If the plant is ISO-certified, one or two third party auditors will come in every six months, plus, the plant gets a second party audit once a year. On our total quality and ISO surveillance audits, we find very few major or minor nonconformances because the internal auditors are catching issues and initiating appropriate corrective action, driving continual improvement."

How to Design and Document an Internal EMS Audit System

You must design and develop an internal EMS audit program that includes the characteristics listed above. After a suitable audit structure is defined, you will need to define the scope, methods, responsibilities, and frequency of reporting for the audits.

Scope

The scope of the audit encompasses policies, practices, procedures, or requirements covered by ISO 14001 and EMS requirements that have been established internally. Note that the EMS audit process focuses on determining the existence and proper functioning of the EMS elements, not their performance.

Methods

The EMS audit methods to be used for collecting information must be identified in the audit procedure. Examples include conducting interviews with personnel, examining documents, and observing performance and activities.

You may be interviewed during an EMS audit.

Responsibilities

Roles and responsibilities for performing EMS audits should be assigned within the audit procedure. Ideally, the auditors should be objective, unbiased, and free from conflict of interest, and independent of the area being audited. Auditors should be competent and possess appropriate knowledge, skills, and experience in auditing methods.

Frequency of Reporting

The EMS audit *procedure* must specify the need to report audit results to management and how these results are to be reported. The EMS audit *schedule* specifies how often audits are to be performed. Usually, EMS audits are more frequent during EMS implementation and early use, and are less frequent as experience is gained and the system is optimized.

Selecting Auditors and Providing Training

The EMS auditors should be drawn from a cross-section of departments and functions in all levels of the organization. There should be enough people on the team for effective audit performance, without the audit being a burden on any one person. Individuals who are selected to serve as EMS auditors need to be trained and mentored so they will have the knowledge, skills, and experience to perform effective EMS audits.

Implementing the EMS Audits

EMS audits should be initiated during the time the EMS is being implemented. This is an advantage because it allows you to:

- Adjust and improve the EMS as it is being developed.
- Provide training to internal auditor staff.
- Help educate all employees on the EMS audit process.
- Generate audit records.

You will need to include a training and education session for managers to explain the purpose of EMS audits, the managers' applications of the results, and the roles managers are expected to perform in responding to audit results. It is critical to the effective functioning of an EMS that audit findings receive timely responses and corrections. ■

Notes

Management reviews must be documented.

Chapter 9
4.6 Management Review

The final part of the *plan, do, check, act* improvement loop is the *act* portion, which is referred to as Management Review in the ISO 14001 standard.

The Standard Requires...

ISO 14001 (4.6) requires that top management review the EMS. The review process needs to *"address the possible need for changes to policy, objectives, and other elements of the environmental management system, in light of environmental management system audit results, changing circumstances, and the commitment to continual improvement."*

The review process must be defined and documented. Management must define how often this is done and what is reviewed. It is expected that the following items will, at a minimum, be reviewed:

- The EMS policy.
- The results of EMS audits and findings.
- The effectiveness of the corrective and preventive action system.
- Performance against established environmental objectives and targets.

The results of these management reviews must be recorded and retained as an environmental record.

Implementation Tasks

The following steps will help you develop and use your management review process:

Design and Document the Management Review Process

Design the management review process. The process could include:

- People involved in management reviews.
- Items to be covered in management review meetings.
- Records to be kept and person responsible for these records.

The process can be documented in a procedure (not required by ISO 14001) that will guide the management team.

Implement the Management Review Process

The management review process can be implemented in two stages. During initial EMS development, the reviews can be performed more frequently and used to drive implementation. Progress reports can be presented along with guidance for resources if needed. After the EMS is in operation, the frequency of reviews can be reduced for maintenance and improvement of the EMS.

Use Management Review Results to Drive EMS Improvement

The management review process can be used to make changes and improvements in the EMS. New objectives and targets and new methods of operation can be drawn from the results and analyzed during management reviews.

9

Milan Management Review Agenda
Combined with CARs, Minutes, Documentation

Tellas explains that Milan Screw Products' system tracks corrective action reports (CARs) as part of the management review process, including minutes of the meeting and documentation to support corrective actions. "The management review group meets quarterly, at a minimum," he states, "and reviews the corrective action reports as part of the agenda. If there is a problem, we attach an action item number to that item. Actions taken to correct the problem are documented and attached to the agenda, and the whole process then becomes the minutes of the meeting, as well as the written record for all of these steps."

Action items on the Milan Screw Products management review agenda and tracking list include all kinds of issues, not just environmental. The company's implementation of ISO 9001:2000 and ISO 14001 management systems has resulted in a better and more integrated tracking system for a wide range of business issues. Tellas points out that handwritten notes are added to the action item tracking sheet as problems are resolved, resulting in complete records of management review agendas, CARs, actions taken, minutes of the meeting, and closure of the issues.

Integrate with Existing Programs and Activities

Examine other review activities to determine whether the EMS management review can be modeled after a successful process already in existence. Most organizations struggle with this aspect of an EMS because it is difficult to step back and examine the perfor-

You may be able to integrate your EMS with existing programs.

mance of the entire system. Because management reviews are a critical function of an EMS, you may want to conduct these separately from other meetings. ■

Figure 9-1 Milan Screw Company Management Review Action Item List

Action Item #	Date	Task	Person
233	3/11/02	CAR #80 Crimp nuts returned with thread damage.	
233	5/30/02	Contractor changed PO to state no washing of parts (to avoid thread damage).	
233	1/21/03	Awaiting contractor action—Manager responsible.	Mary
233	4/2/03	Contractor doing a cost analysis on rack vs. barrel plate, cost effectiveness of design.	Contractor
233	5/27/03	Action still pending with contractor—low priority with customer.	Contractor
Safety Management			
285	12/8/02	Safety program updated.	Barbara
286	12/8/02	Lift truck training completed except for sky-lift training, which is needed.	Barbara
287	12/8/02	Employee has repetitive motion injury. Process changed to eliminate the repetitive lifting. Employee still on limited duty.	Chuck
Environmental Management			
269	6/12/02	CAR #106 Unlabeled containers found	Chuck
	1/21/03	during walk-around. Materials discarded or labeled. CLOSED.	
270	6/12/02	CAR #107 Several materials found with no	Chuck
	7/15/02	MSDSs. MSDSs ordered and posted. CLOSED.	
288	12/8/02	Environmental training needed.	Tom
289	12/8/02	Update of environmental program needed.	Chuck
Quality Management			
251	4/9/02	Quality system is functional and adequate, although not without opportunities for improvement.	
255	5/28/02	Consolidation of spreadsheet needed—Excel	Mary
256	5/28/02	Quality training update needed.	Chuck
267	6/12/02	CAR #104 Audit finding illegible—audit results unclear.	Linda
	1/21/03	*Procedure changed. CLOSED.*	
268	6/12/03	CAR #105 No documentation of audit notification. Manual changed. CLOSED.	Linda

Notes

A BP production pad in Alaska.

10

Chapter 10
The Certification Process

After you have implemented an EMS based on the ISO 14001 standard, you may want a third party to independently certify that your EMS conforms to the standard. This process is known as registering or certifying the EMS to the standard.

The certification is performed by a *registrar* that has been *accredited* by an accreditation body that is approved by the International Organization for Standardization. An accreditation body accredits (approves) a registrar as competent to perform ISO 14001 certification of environmental management systems.

The authors spoke with two registrars about the certification process, Advanced Waste Management (AWM) and Bureau Veritas Quality International (BVQI).

Advanced Waste Management Systems (AWM) was established as a registrar in 1985 and has offices in Chattanooga, Tennessee; Milwaukee, Wisconsin; Boston; New Orleans; Boise, Idaho; and Bucharest, Romania. To date, AWM has issued 133 certifications to ISO 14001, the Occupational Health and Safety Assessment Standard (OHSAS) 18001, and some conformance certifications to show that the organization meets the requirements of the standard but is not pursuing official certification. Recent clients include Astra-Evangalista in Buenos Aires, Argentina; ARC Rocket Motors (for missiles and satellites); Fujisawa Health Care (pharmaceuticals); and Montenay Dutchess Waste Energy, a trash-burning power plant.

Bureau Veritas Quality International (BVQI) has certified 265 sites to ISO 14001 in North America, although some of these are multiple sites. BVQI has offices in 60 countries and works in over 100 countries. It employs more than 2,000 experienced auditors, and works through multinational networks. Accredited by 30 accreditation bodies, BVQI has assisted over 50,000 companies worldwide to achieve certification to ISO 9000 and ISO 14001, as well as other equivalent standards.

In the United States, registrars are accredited by the Registrar Accreditation Board (RAB). The registrars are required to use RAB-certified EMS auditors to conduct the ISO 14001 certification audits. The registrar performs an independent assessment of your EMS, but cannot consult or provide advice on how to design and implement your EMS, as this would be a conflict of interest. Likewise, a consultant that helps with the design and implementation of your EMS cannot certify that it meets the ISO 14001 standard.

What the Registrar Can Tell You

Richard Ellis, CEO of AWM, states that the registrar is able to tell people at a company what things they will need to look at in the audit. He notes that a company may say what it has or has not done and ask if this would be a major nonconformance. At this point, the registrar can say whether it is a major nonconformance, as there is no point in doing the audit if the company is not ready. He adds that he can answer yes or no questions, but he can't say how to fix it, adding that any registrar who explains how to correct a noncompliance is consulting.

Dave Church of BVQI says that BVQI, like many other registrars, offers a pre-assessment audit—a practice audit—that about 75 percent of its clients use. In this way, the company gets a chance to look at its system to be sure everything is there, and BVQI gets a chance to look at the company's system and to note nonconformances. The practice audit also allows the employees to more closely understand the audit process.

Selecting a Registrar

The organization seeking certification of its EMS pays the registrar to perform the audit. You will want to select a registrar once you have decided to seek certification.

Items you should consider when selecting a registrar:

- Is the registrar accredited?
- Do your customers require you to use a specific registrar?

Evaluate several registrars before selecting one.

- Does the registrar have experience with your industry?

RAB provides a list of approved registrars that are accredited to perform certification audits in the United States. RAB will not recommend one registrar over another. This means that you will need to interview several registrars, determine what industries they are familiar with, obtain references from their customers, and compare prices. You will also want to review the qualifications of the registrar's auditors. You should take time to do this carefully, as you are entering a relationship that will likely last many years.

Because BP is a very large organization with a complex business configuration, Norman Ingram says they approached certification to ISO 14001 with a fairly rigorous project planning methodology. They conducted several internal EMS audits leading up to certification, inviting an auditor from DNV (Det Norske Veritas—their registrar) to sit in on one of the internal audits. This gave the auditor a chance to learn about their organization. Ingram says it is important to lay the groundwork well in advance about the intensity of detail that will occur in the audit so employees view the audit process in a positive light.

Checking Out a Registrar

Ellis encourages companies to make sure a registrar is "clean," that is, that he has no competing interest, such as an ISO consulting arm. "This is an irrefutable conflict of interest. When there are conflicting interests, the credibility of that registrar is extremely suspect," he notes. "Sooner or later, there will be an environmental catastrophe or an accident, and, as an ISO-registered company, it's going to come into question what kinds of conflict of interest the registrar had. It's the Arthur Andersen situation all over again."

Talk with the companies that the registrars have certified to find out what kind of job the registrar did for them. Many registrars, such as AWM, have a list of clients and contact people on their web site.

To find a registrar, Church recommends compiling a list of registrars and then calling their clients to find out what they are like to work with. If clients are not listed on the registrar's web site, ask for a client list and the registrar will send it to you. He warns that there is very little standardization on quoting charges, which has led more companies to ask for all-inclusive rates, which are difficult but not impossible for the registrar to provide, as travel costs are hard to estimate. He recommends trying to fix the cost as closely as possible, plus travel. Environmental auditors have to travel from the offices where they are based, while quality management auditors are plentiful throughout the United States.

There are several steps involved with ISO 14001 certification:
- Pre-assessment audit
- Document review
- Certification audit
- Surveillance audit

Pre-Assessment Audit

To determine if you are ready for the certification audit, you will need to do a pre-assessment audit (also called a pre-certification audit). This is typically performed by the registrar. It gives you an opportunity to meet with the registrar and to understand what he will be looking for.

The registrar will visit your facility, interview key staff and determine your certification readiness. He may find that your EMS is immature and may be months away from being fully implemented. He will recommend that you postpone the certification audit until a later date. On the other hand, the registrar may find that your system is mature and ready for a third party audit, and set a mutually acceptable time with you for the certification audit.

The pre-assessment audit will help your employees understand the certification process and the role of the third party auditor. The pre-assessment audit should not come as a surprise to your employees as they should have experienced at least one, and ideally more than one, internal EMS audit before this time. The pre-assessment audit typically takes place over a couple of days and is commonly performed by the registrar's lead auditor.

Document Review

The registrar will review your EMS documentation before the certification audit. This will be done either at your site or (more typically) at the registrar's office. The registrar will want to review your environmental policy, EMS manual, document control process, and corrective action procedures, as well as other requested EMS documents.

The registrar is checking whether your EMS documents have addressed all the requirements of ISO 14001. If certain documents appear to be inadequate or absent, the registrar may postpone the certification audit until any document deficiencies are corrected.

Certification Audit

Following a successful pre-assessment audit and document review, you will be ready for the certification audit. An audit team, consisting of one or more auditors and a lead auditor, will spend several days at your facility. They will interview managers, supervisors, and employees on their awareness of and involvement with the EMS. They will be trying to determine if your EMS meets the requirements of ISO 14001 and whether you are following your own EMS procedures. It important for everyone to understand that your *system* is being audited, *not* individual performance.

Quelling Audit Jitters

"There should be nothing to prepare for," Dave Church states. "If employees are doing their jobs and following procedures, they will simply get caught doing what is right." He adds that it is important to tell employees what will happen, and what the auditors expect.

The length of the audit and number of auditors on the team will be a function of the size of your operation. It may vary from two auditors spending two days on site (4 person days) to four auditors spending three days on site (12 person days). The price will be based on the number of person days and should not vary significantly between registrars.

Major and Minor Nonconformances

Randy Daugharthy, President of BVQI North America, explains that any nonconformances observed will be documented by the audit team. Each nonconformance is classified as either major or minor. A major is written when an element of the standard has not been implemented, or there is a systemic problem within the EMS causing a significant weakness. A minor is written when an isolated glitch in the system is observed. An example of a minor might be a record that is not filled out properly, a work instruction that was not followed completely, or a document that has not been controlled as required.

A major nonconformance will require a revisit by the lead auditor to verify that the corrective action has been implemented. A minor may be cleared onsite, via fax, mail, or e-mail. The auditor must review the objective evidence that the necessary corrective action has been taken before clearing the nonconformance.

After the audit has been completed and nonconformances have been cleared, all audit paperwork is submitted by the lead auditor for an independent review by another designated employee of the registrar. If all work is approved, a certificate indicating that the EMS meets ISO 14001 can be issued to the company.

There are three possible outcomes from the certification audit:

1. Your system conforms to ISO 14001. The registrar will grant certification.

2. Your system has minor nonconformances with ISO 14001. Certification will be granted contingent upon your correcting the nonconformances within a specified time frame.

3. Your system has major nonconformances with ISO 14001. You will not be granted certification and will be told to correct all nonconformances before being re-audited.

Be Prepared for Certification!

Richard Ellis has some advice for employees to follow during the audit: "They need to know exactly what their assignments are under the EMS. It's also important not to scare employees. If an employee says, 'I'm not sure' or 'I think' it will make the auditor pursue harder." He notes that the certifying organizations and auditors need to maintain a sense of humor about the audit, rather than become intense, which can happen and is not productive.

"Most companies are ready and will get certified, in fact, about 85 percent," Ellis continues. "The registrar should go in with some sense that the company is ready and not with some idea that employees are trying to hide some kind of major non-conformance. Some registrars feel they must find a non-conformance, which can create an adversarial relationship. It's important to trust the registrar to be fair, and realize the registrar is not a grand inquisitor."

Celebration at the Port of Houston!

The port authority was so pleased with its certification that it had a certification party, complete with tee shirts and a huge banner across the front of the administration building. The port plans to extend ISO 14001 EMS implementation throughout the port, with the Galveston container terminal next on the list. An ISO 14001 EMS is also being developed for the engineering department.

Surveillance Audits

Certification does not end with the certification audit. To keep your certification, the registrar will perform periodic surveillance audits to ensure that your EMS is being maintained, typically every six months following initial certification. Each of these is not a comprehensive audit of the entire EMS but focuses on specific elements such as document control, corrective action, or management review. The entire EMS is audited every three years following the initial certification audit. ∎

Getting Better and Better

Paul Steucke points out that Ft. Lewis got to its implementation through advertising with posters, cards, awareness training, e-mails—thoroughly saturating everyone about ISO 14001. "However, as we got close to certification, we got nervous. We wanted to put it off because we felt we weren't ready. A consultant worked with us and pointed out that ISO 14001 is the floor, not the ceiling. You get all the pieces and parts in place, and from there, you use continual improvement to get better."

Notes 10

A herd of caribou grazes near a BP rig in Alaska.

11

Chapter 11
Some Continual Improvement Insights

"Certification to ISO 14001 isn't something you do and then you are finished and don't have to think about it any more. It really doesn't work that way. The easy bit is certification. The challenge is maintaining certification through continual improvement and monitoring a rigorous compliance focus."

— **Norman Ingram, BP**

Continual improvement is an ongoing process that involves everyone in your organization. There are two elements of continual improvement: (1) changes that result in better processes, and (2) maintenance of the system.

When continual improvement becomes part of an organization—for example, as a part of its EMS—it is easier to talk about than to carry out. For example, how can you develop a culture that encourages change and improvement every day? Enthusiasm for the EMS will subside once you have achieved certification. Management may consider that you have reached your goal and that's it! However, improved environmental performance will only be achieved through continual improvement. You may be given a list of reasons why you can't make improvements:

- It's not in the budget.
- It's a good idea, but the timing is bad.

- This isn't company policy.
- It isn't our business; let someone else think about it.
- It's not improvement; it's common sense.

This happens all the time. Without ideas and suggestions for improvement, your EMS will stagnate. Management may address the problem with short term solutions, such as investing in new machinery, changing the facility layout or hiring consultants to study the problem. However, these changes will not alter management's attitude towards continual improvement. This is why top management commitment is essential for a successful EMS. Without such support, continual improvement is not possible.

Milan Screw Products made a move from a 14,000-square-foot plant to a 34,000-square-foot plant an opportunity to apply continual improvement principles to eliminate some environmental aspects of their business.

Designing Out Environmental Aspects

Tellas explains, "Many of the things that showed up as aspects at our old building have been designed out of the new building. Oil that soaked into the old concrete floors is no longer a problem, as our new plant has non-porous floors sealed with epoxy. We also have a much more efficient oil mist collection system to collect the oil with electrostatic precipitators and put it back into the machines for re-use."

"We found that heating the oil was reducing its life. Instead of heating oil to 150° and collecting it in a sump in the base of the machine that recycles the oil, we changed to a central coolant system. The oil falls into a flume in the floor along with chips—steel turnings—where the oil is centrifugally separated from the chips. The oil is filtered out very well and returned to the

machines. The dry steel turnings are blown out and hauled away as a raw material for steel smelting." Tellas adds that the machines don't generate nearly as much heat as before, and says they still spill some oil on the floor, but don't track it much because of the new floors. They also filter all the oil in a central system and not just in a machine.

The concerns of neighbors at the old Milan plant were thoroughly addressed at the new, larger plant. One of the first concerns at the old site was noise. "In our new site," Tellas explains, "no one even knows we are here because we are so quiet, compared to a nearby stamping plant in the industrial park. Smell is no longer an issue because of the new electrostatic precipitators, and fire far less an issue because our new plant has a sprinkler system. Visual appeal that was lacking in the old plant is not a problem in the new one. We also placed an impermeable layer of clay under portions of our floor, in addition to a thick-walled metal flume with weld joints inspected for liquid-tightness that is encased in concrete, to greatly reduce our concerns about oil migration through the soil."

Milan's new plant eliminates many aspects of the old plant.

Baxter International, with more than 100 sites all over the world, preaches continual improvement so that all of its plants can achieve the same level of environmental protection through the ISO 14001 EMS.

Continual Improvement as a Leveler of Regs

Baxter International's Irish facility is subject to complex and detailed environmental regulations that may result in a greater level of environmental protection than that experienced in the Baxter facility in Costa Rica. However, the continual improvement requirement of ISO 14001 will likely lead to the two EMSs providing comparable levels of protection over time.

For example, the Costa Rica facility could decide to evaluate sulfates in wastewater, checking with the World Health Organization to determine the maximum level, which would then result in improved environmental protection. It should be noted that all sites must adhere to Baxter's EHS policies, such as World Health Organization standards for drinking water, no matter where the site is located or who supplies the water.

Continual improvement offers the potential for true improvements by bringing together resources, ideas, knowledge, and expertise. Everyone has something to offer. There is always something that can be improved upon.

Although Milan was able to eliminate many aspects by moving to a new plant, the employees and General Manager continue to refine their improvements still more.

"This process change means that the coolant doesn't just stay in the machine, getting dirtier and dirtier and hotter and hotter," Tellas adds. "The coolant stays much cleaner; we just add anti-wear properties or anti-oxidant properties as needed."

action items

Continual Improvement

- Do not make excuses. Question current practices.
- Discard conventional ideas.
- Think of how to do it, not why it cannot be done.
- Look for root causes to problems.
- Do not seek perfection; make a start.

Continual improvement is built into the ISO 14001 standard. The need to make a commitment to continual improvement in the environmental policy, the setting of objectives and targets, auditing of the EMS, and management review all lead to continual improvement of the EMS. ∎

Milan's Improvements

Tellas of Milan Screw Products explains that OSHA's requirement for oil mist is 5 mg. per cubic meter. "At the worst portion of our old shop," he points out, "we had 2 mg. per cubic meter. In most of the shop area of our new plant, we have 0.5 mg. per cubic meter. We have one place that approaches 1 mg. per cubic meter, where there is an eddy between two air make-up units, but we are working on this to get it down to the level of the rest of the shop."

Milan bought a new air compressor with an oil-water separator for the condensate that allowed them to dispose of the water in the sanitary sewer instead of putting it in with the manifested waste. "We have a little test kit to make sure there is no oil in the water," Chuck Tellas explains. "This worked very well. It wasn't a big money-saver but we were able to reduce the waste going out our door. There are some other areas where we need to do that, one of which is mop water. We tried an ultra-filtration unit and had quite a bit of trouble with it. The thing just kept plugging up." He adds that it is a goal in the future to further reduce waste streams.

Ironically, one engineering improvement added an aspect in the form of media from the company's vacuum-bed paper filter. Tellas explains, "Normally, with our type of machinery, there is a sump at the bottom of the machine that holds 100 to 150 gallons of cutting oil that is constantly recirculated within the machine. What we have done is to cut a hole in the bottom of all the machines so it falls out and is directed in a flume to a filter where many of the particulates are filtered out. The coolant then goes back into the machine. We built a little cradle to dry the filter when it comes out, as it still had some oil in it. We squeeze the oil out of it, so that the waste goes out as solid waste."

BP's Long Range Objectives and Targets

"Our underlying objectives don't change that much," Norman Ingram explains. *"We want to reduce impacts to air and water, to minimize waste, and to reduce impacts to wildlife and habitat. Our targets are a combination of several inputs and an annual bottoms-up look at our environmental aspects, focusing on the significant aspects locally. We combine these with input and guidance from our corporate headquarters around some of the more macro issues, such as greenhouse gas emissions. BP has taken some fairly enlightened approaches to these topics where we are setting global goals."*

As a company, BP took on the spirit of the ten-year goals of the Kyoto Agreement, which were to return to the greenhouse gas emissions to the levels of 1990. The company was able to accomplish this goal in four years. BP is involved in a strategy to move to gas instead of oil as a more sought-after, environmentally friendly fuel. The company is also involved in alternative energy sources, and is the largest solar energy company in the world. It also works with wind-generated power. Almost all the power generated for the Olympic Village and its supporting infrastructure in Sydney, Australia was solar power supplied by BP.

Meshing ISO 14001 and OHSAS 18001

Richard Ellis of AWM says he is seeing an increased level of integration of standards. "Almost every client we have has the same people managing environment and safety and health. There is nearly always an EHS or an ESH department, so it's a natural to integrate the safety and health standards with ISO 14001. The Occupational Health and Safety Assessment Series (OHSAS) 18001 standard is written in perfect parallel to ISO 14001, so meshing the two is very logical. Most of the time, the driver for integration is a directive from corporate headquarters in an effort to manage risk, control expenses, and avoid bad publicity and poor worker safety and health practices. There is recognition that the management system model really works."

Long-Range Continual Improvement

Paul Steucke at Ft. Lewis plans to expand his work with the EMS from public works to the garrison level, and then installation-wide. "The EMS is really great and has continual improvement built into it, but it doesn't tell you how much continual improvement to apply. You can take baby steps and still be certified. Our 25 year goals are things like reducing air emissions from traffic sources by 85%, and having zero net waste by 2025. We plan to recover all listed and candidate federal species in the South Puget Sound area by 2017."

Notes

Appendix A
Glossary

Accreditation: The qualifications of a registrar that grant the authority to conduct third-party audits of an organization's environmental management system and to grant certification to that organization for conformance to the ISO 14001 standard.

Assessment: The equivalent of an in-house audit conducted by personnel within an organization, an environmental consulting firm, or a registrar to determine the degree of alignment of the environmental management system with ISO 14001 criteria set by the organization.

Audit Team: A trained, qualified group of people from an organization that conducts assessments or audits for conformance to that organization's environmental management system standard criteria.

Certification: Status achieved when an organization has been audited to a voluntary management system, such as ISO 14001, by an accredited third party, usually a registrar, to conformance to the standard, and has met the criteria. Certification and registration are used interchangeably.

Compliance: Adherence to the regulatory and legislative requirements of state, federal, and local agencies as required by law. Not to be confused with conformance, which applies only to ISO 14001.

Conformance: Alignment with the requirements of ISO 14001, a voluntary standard. For greater clarity, the authors use compliance only when speaking of adherence to regulatory and legislative requirements.

Continual Improvement: Enhancements of the environmental management system that are instituted on an ongoing basis through the checking and corrective action process, and through improvements in environmental performance as required by the environmental policy.

Contractor: An organization performing work on a contractual basis for another organization as a supplier or in performing specific work, which may occur on the site of the hiring organization.

Corrective Action: Steps taken to correct processes or activities within the environmental management system as observed in frequent routine checks at all levels and departments or through internal or external audits. Corrective actions can be written as Corrective Action Reports (CARs).

Ecolabeling: The Type I, Type II, and Type III labels of the ISO standard for products that (a) have been awarded labels under a national third party labeling program; (b) self-declaration environmental claims by the manufacturer; and (c) environmental information profiles. Products may bear more than one kind of label.

Environmental Aspect: An activity, product, or service of an organization that has the potential to affect the environment.

Environmental Impact: The resulting positive or negative effect on the environment from an organization's activities, products, or services.

Environmental Management System (EMS): A system made up of the organizational structure, planning, responsibilities, processes, procedures, practices, and resources supporting the development, implementation, achievement, review, and maintenance of the environmental policy.

Environmental Management System Audit: A focused, documented process to determine the level of conformance of an organization's environmental management system to EMS requirements. This process includes a report of audit results to management.

Environmental Objective: An environmental management goal to be achieved that is set by the organization and is based on the environmental policy. Objectives are quantified when possible.

Environmental Policy: An organization's statement of its environmental performance intentions and principles. The policy creates a framework for activities and sets environmental objectives and targets.

Environmental Target: An EMS performance requirement that is based on the environmental policy and is quantified when possible. Targets that have been set must be met for the organization to achieve its objectives.

Joint Assessment: Two concurrent assessments performed as one integrated audit of the criteria for two management system standards, such as ISO 9001 or ISO 9002 and ISO 14001 (quality and environmental).

Input: Raw materials and energy that go into the manufacture of a product.

Life Cycle: The stages of a product, from raw material to development of the product, to ultimate recycling or disposal of the product as waste.

Life-Cycle Assessment or LCA: The analysis of a product or service through all stages of its life cycle in terms of raw material and energy use, manufacturing, transportation, product use, maintenance, and waste management.

Nonconformance: A process or activity that is found to be out of alignment with the ISO 14001 EMS through the routine checking and corrective action process, an internal assessment, or a certification or surveillance audit performed by the registrar.

Output: Products and wastes resulting from the manufacturing process.

Prevention of Pollution: Processes, practices, materials, and products that effectively avoid, reduce, or control pollution. Examples of prevention of pollution controls include recycling, energy conservation, and process or materials changes.

Procedure: An organization's established and documented process for performing a specific activity.

Registration: See Certification.

Subcontractor: An organization that provides a product or service to a contractor on a contractual basis.

Supplier: An organization providing a product to another organization. In this handbook, a supplier is an organization that provides a product to the organization that is implementing or has implemented ISO 14001.

Surveillance Audits: Audits performed by the registrar at regular intervals, typically about every six months, after certification to check the EMS for conformance to ISO 14001. Each surveillance audit focuses on specific elements of the standard, resulting in a complete audit of all EMS elements every three years.

Third Party: An organization that is independent of organizations involved in the manufacture and sale of a product. In this handbook, the third party is the registrar.

Waste: A useless byproduct left over from the manufacture of a product. ■

Appendix A

Notes

Notes

Notes

Appendix B
Resources: Contributors, Standards, and Websites

Contributors

Advanced Waste Management (AWM)

AWM (registrar)
6430 Hixson Pike
P.O. Box 100
Hixson, TN 37343

Website .... *http://www.awm.net*

Contact .... Richard Ellis, Ph.D.
Title .... Chairman and President
Phone .... (423) 843-2206
Fax .... (423) 843-2310
E-mail .... *ellis@awm.net*

American Council for an Energy-Efficient Economy (ACEEE)

1001 Connecticut Avenue NW, Suite 801
Washington, D.C. 20036-5525

Website .... *http://www.GreenerCars.com*

Contact .... Jim Kliesch
Title .... Research Associate
Phone .... (202) 429-8873, Ext. 721
Fax .... (202) 429-0507
E-mail .... *greenercars@aceee.org*

Baxter International, Inc.

Baxter International, Inc.
One Baxter Parkway, DF 4-3W
Deerfield, IL 60015-4633
Website .... *http://www.baxter.com*

Contact .... Mike Cycyota
Title .... Director of Corporate EHS Audits
Phone .... (847) 948-3621
Fax .... (847) 948-4114
E-mail .... *mike_a_cycyota@baxter.com*

Baxter International, Inc.
One Baxter Parkway, DF 4-3E
Deerfield, IL 60015-4633
Website .... *http://www.baxter.com*

Contact .... Ricardo Valverde
Title .... Manager, Environmental Health and Safety
Phone .... (847) 948-2648
Fax .... (847) 948-3602
E-mail .... *ricardo_valverde@baxter.com*

BP Exploration Alaska Inc.

BP Exploration Alaska Inc.
900 East Benson Blvd.
P.O. Box 196612
Anchorage, AK 99519-6612
Website .... *http://www.bp.com*

Contact .... Norman Ingram
Title .... Manager, Compliance Assurance and
                  Continual Improvement
Phone .... (907) 564-4798
Fax .... (907) 564-5003
E-mail .... *ingramn@bp.com*

Appendix B

Bureau Veritas Quality International (BVQI)

BVQI (registrar)
515 West 5th Street
Jamestown, NY 14701

Website .... *http://www.bvqina.com*

Contact .... Dave Church
Title .... EMS Director for BVQI
Phone .... (716) 484-9004, Ext. 106
Fax .... (716) 664-7588
E-mail .... *dchurch@bvqina.com*

Milan Screw Products, Inc.

Milan Screw Products, Inc.
291 Squires Drive
P.O. Box 180
Milan, MI 48160-0180

Website .... *http://www.mscrew.com*

Contact .... Chuck Tellas
Title .... Owner and CEO
Phone .... (734) 439-2431
Fax .... (734) 439-1040
E-mail .... *ctellas@ix.netcom.com*

Port of Houston Authority

Port of Houston Authority
111 East Loop North
P. O. Box 2562
Houston, TX 77252-2562

Website .... *http://www.portofhouston.com*

Contact .... Laura Fiffick, CSP
Title .... Environmental Affairs Manager
Phone .... (713) 670-2438
Fax .... (713) 670-2427
E-mail .... *lfiffick@poha.com*

Trus Joist, A Weyerhaeuser Company

Trus Joist
P.O. Box 5326
Valdosta, GA 31603-5326

Website .... *http://www.trusjoist.com*

Contact .... Allan Ricketts
Title .... Quality Systems Manager, Manufacturing Operations
Phone .... (800) 448-8921, Ext. 241
Fax .... (229) 247-2995
E-mail .... *ricketa@trusjoist.com*

United States Army, Ft. Lewis, Washington

U.S. Army, Ft. Lewis, Washington AFVH-P.O., MS 14
Box 339500
Ft. Lewis, WA 98433-9500

Website: .... *http://www.lewis.army.mil*

Contact .... Paul Steucke
Title .... Chief, Environmental and Natural Resources Division
Phone .... (253) 966-1760
Fax .... (253) 966-4985
E-mail .... *steuckep@lewis.army.mil*

Standards Publications

The ISO 14000 series of standards is copyrighted. Individual standards may be purchased from any one of the following organizations.

American National Standards Institute (ANSI)

25 West 43rd Street, 4th Floor
New York, NY 10036
Phone .... (212) 642-4980
Fax .... (212) 302-1286
Website .... *http://www.ansi.org/cat_b.html*
E-mail .... *ansionline@ansi.org*

Appendix B

American Society for Testing and Materials (ASTM)

ASTM Customer Service
100 Barr Harbor Drive
West Conshohocken, PA 19248-2959
Phone .... (610) 832-9585
Fax .... (610) 832-9555
Website .... *http://www.astm.org/e-order.html*
E-mail .... *service@local.astm.org*

American Society for Quality (ASQ)

600 North Plankinton Avenue
P. O. Box 3005
Milwaukee, WI 53201-3005
Phone .... (800) 248-1946
Fax .... (414) 272-1734
Website .... *http://www.asq.org*
E-mail .... *asqc@asqc.org*

NSF International

789 N. Dixboro Road
P.O. Box 130140
Ann Arbor, MI 48113-0140
Phone .... (800) NSF-MARK
Fax .... (313) 769-0109
Website .... *http://www.nsf.org/publications/ems.html*
E-mail .... *info@nsf.org*

Websites

American National Standards Institute (ANSI)

http://www.ansi.org

As an administrator and coordinator of voluntary management systems for private industry in the United States, ANSI is the official US representative to TC 207. ANSI is a private, non-profit membership organization supported by public and private organizations, with a primary goal of enhancing the competitiveness of US business through the promotion of voluntary consensus standards.

CEEM Inc.

http://www.ceem.com

Provides ISO 9000, ISO 14000, and QS 9000 training and information. CEEM is the publisher of *International Environmental Systems Update (IESU)* newsletter, which provides trends and market analysis on ISO 14001, and *Pro Bono*, a newsletter on strategic philanthropy. A new feature of this website is *IESU Online*, which is available to readers who subscribe to the newsletter.

The Center for Intelligent Information Retrieval

http://ciir.cs.umass.edu

Allows retrieval and search of environmental, safety, and health requirements, and includes the *United States Code*, most of the *Code of Federal Regulations*, and the *Federal Register*.

Corporate Environmental Strategy: The Journal of Environmental Leadership

http://www.corporate-env-strategy.com
Corporate Environmental Strategy (CES) is a quarterly publication that focuses on the connection between strategic environmental management and sound business strategy, emphasizing how profitability and sustainability can be achieved while moving beyond regulatory and liability issues.

Eco-Compass

http://www.islandpress.org/eco-compass/

Lists news and useful environmental websites on the Internet, a service of Island Press, a nonprofit publisher of environmental books. This is a good tool for anyone who wants to stay abreast of current environmental resources.

Environment Daily

http://www.environmentdaily.com

Addresses major environmental news and issues in the European Union. Four weekly issues are available on a trial basis; then the reader must pay for a subscription. The e-mail newsletter can be tailored to deliver only the news in your areas of interest.

Environment in Asia

http://www.asianenviro.com

This site provides comprehensive information on environmental news, policies, and markets in the Asia-Pacific region. Countries included are Japan, China, Hong Kong, Taiwan, South Korea, Malaysia, Thailand, the Philippines, Indonesia, Singapore, Vietnam, India, Sri Lanka, Brunei, and Cambodia/Laos/Myanmar.

Environmental Expert

http://www.environmentalexpert.com

Provides news and articles, as well as a list of business and scientific periodicals by topic. Click on a title and you get a list of sample articles in a pdf format for that title, each of which can be opened and printed. There is a catalog of 1,200 book titles worldwide, searchable by subject or keyword, any of which can be purchased online. Also included are listings of events, professional services, training resources, environmental software, featured storefronts, technology and equipment, and job listings.

Environmental Management Systems: An Implementation Guide for Small and Medium-Sized Organizations

http://www.epa.gov/ebtpages/environmentalmanagement.html
With a focus on ISO 14001 voluntary environmental management systems, the EPA provides documents in three formats that contain an EMS toolkit, sample environmental policies, and other elements of ISO 14001.

Environmentally Oriented Pages from the Quality Network

http://www.quality.co.uk/ecoadvic.htm
This site provides a variety of general information about ISO 14000, along with an overview of the standard and comparisons of ISO 14000 (international) to BS 7750 (British), and the Eco Management and Audit Scheme (EMAS) (European).

EurekAlert!

http://www.eurekalert.org
Produced by the American Association for the Advancement of Science with technical support provided by Stanford University, this website is a news-server for up-to-date research in science, medicine, and engineering.

Globus Registry

http://www.worldpreferred.com
Published by World Preferred, the Globus Registry is the definitive database of Globus Class organizations and companies that have been certified to a recognized quality or environmental management standard (ISO 9000, QS 9000, ISO 14001), by an authorized, accredited registrar. Has excellent search capability for environmental issues.

GreenBiz

http://www.greenbiz.com

A free weekly e-newsletter with current environmental news and features, job openings, tools to use in searching for an environmental job, an online bookstore, an events calendar, links to key environmental sites, and listings of new university courses on business and the environment.

Green Seal

http://www.greenseal.org

Green Seal is one of 25 different national labeling programs for Type I labels, which are third party labeling programs.

International Organization for Standardization

http://www.iso.ch

An electronic information service provided by the Central Secretariat of the International Organization for Standardization in Geneva, Switzerland, this site provides a catalog of ISO standards, late-breaking news, a listing of technical committees and their meeting schedules, and the history and structure of the organization.

A Librarian's Guide to EPA Resources on the Web

http://www.epa.gov/glnpo/ala/liblinks/topics/websites.html

Search a variety of databases, including the Enviroene collection of databases that encompass pollution prevention, compliance assurance, and enforcement information. Using the search function, the authors found a listing of more than 40,000 environmental articles, including 1,088 on "cost savings."

Regional Environmental Center for Central and Eastern Europe

http://www.rec.org

A nonprofit, international organization with its main office in Szentendre, Hungary, REC promotes cooperation among the many environmental groups in Central and Eastern Europe to develop solutions to environmental problems. This site contains several databases and current environmental news and reports.

Registrar Accreditation Board (RAB)

http://www.rabnet.com

The RAB website offers searchable databases to search for RAB-approved ISO 9000 and ISO 14000 registrars, training course providers, and individual auditors. The site contains specific sections devoted entirely to ISO 9001 quality management systems and to ISO 14001 environmental management systems. There is also a News sections and a News and Notes quarterly newsletter.

Sustainable Business.com

http://www.sustainablebusiness.com

In addition to articles and stock prices, provides a listing of green jobs in North America and Europe; business connections for vendors, partners, and distributors; upcoming events and trade shows; and a sustainable business reference library.

The Morning Tide and Ebb Tide

http://www.tidepool.org

Daily and weekly e-mail newsletters that report primarily on Northwest environmental issues. National and international environmental news are also covered through major news sources, such as the Washington Post, BBC, the Christian Science Monitor, and CNN.

United States Environmental Protection Agency (USEPA)

http://www.epa.gov

The EPA website provides a list of environmental laws and regulations, news and events, publications, locations of offices and EPA libraries, projects, databases, and information for business and industry. ■

Appendix B

Notes

PHOTO CREDIT: BETTY HAGEMAN

Index

Advanced Waste Management Systems (AWMS), Registrar 109-110, 111, 113, 117, 128

American Council for an Energy-Efficient Economy (ACEEE) 8-9

audit program 87, 92, 96

audits, internal 71-72, 92, 97-100, 103, 112

audits, pre-assessment 111, 113, 114-115

audits, third party 57, 97-98, 114-116

awareness programs 44, 47, 67-71, 83, 118

BP Exploration Alaska 16-18, 70-71, 77, 89-90, 112, 121, 127

BVQI (Registrar) 110, 111, 116

Baxter International 15-16, 45, 70, 74, 82, 92, 123-124

calibration 88-89, 96

certification 11, 13, 16-17, 18-20, 28, 75, 109-118

chemicals 57, 83

communications
    external 43, 73-74, 75, 84, 96, 123
    internal 43, 47-49, 52, 72, 82, 84, 96

compliance (with regulations) 7, 10, 36, 43, 48, 53, 58, 74-75, 88-90

conformances (with the standard) 90, 111

continual improvement 21, 43, 94-95, 98, 103, 118, 121-128

contractors 16, 62, 69, 70, 82, 90, 106

corrective and preventive actions 37, 72, 87, 91-93, 96, 98, 103, 105, 114, 117 customers 11, 16

Department of Defense (DOD) 21

document control 21, 65, 78-80, 92, 114, 117

documentation 43, 57, 60, 75-77, 78, 83-84, 88, 93, 97, 103, 105, 114

EMS core team *See steering committee.*

EMS implementation 52

EMS implementation checklist 39-40

EMS manual 76-84, 114

ecolabeling 29-30

economic impact of EMS 9-10, 11, 13, 51, 52, 57-58, 61-62, 74, 126

emergency preparedness and response 65, 83, 84

emissions 8, 36, 57, 127, 128

energy savings 62

environmental aspects 10, 31, 37-38, 50, 53-58, 70, 80, 81, 96, 122, 126

environmental impacts 9-10, 53-58, 75, 82, 127

environmental labeling 29-30

environmental management programs 61

environmental management system (EMS) standards 25-32

environmental management system (EMS) audit *See audit.*

environmental objectives 43, 50, 51, 59-62, 71, 87, 96, 103-104

environmental performance 10-11, 17-18, 48, 66, 89, 121

environmental policy 37, 43-49, 52, 69, 74, 81, 98, 103, 114

environmental responsibility 10-11, 48

environmental targets 18, 43, 50, 59-62, 71, 87, 96, 103-104, 127

Ft. Lewis, WA 20-21, 118, 128

global warming 8

government agencies and ISO 14000 32

greenhouse gases 9, 12, 127

implementation 11, 37, 49, 65, 104, 118

input 31, 127

integration of
  corrective and preventive actions 93
  documentation 81

monitoring systems 88

systems 105, 128

training 68

ISO Standards 23

and government agencies 32

development of 24

history 24-25

purchasing App. B

use of 4

labeling *See ecolabeling.*

legal requirements 50, 58-59

life cycle 31

life-cycle assessment (LCA) 30-31

management review 37, 96, 103-106

management commitment and support 43, 52, 60, 65-66, 100, 103, 122, 127

Milan Screw Products 18, 44, 46, 105-106, 122-123, 126

monitoring and measurement 87-90

noncompliance (to regulations) 91

nonconformances (to the standard) 87, 90-93, 97, 111, 116, 117

Occupational Health and Safety Assessment Standard (OHSAS)18001 109

operational control 65, 80-81

output 31

permits 16, 89

Plan-Do-Check-Act 4, 9, 103

planning 37, 51-61

pollution 54

Port of Houston 19, 47- 49, 69, 75, 117

quality management systems 24-25, 28, 38, 52, 93, 105-106

records 71, 78, 87, 92, 96, 104

recycling 12, 48

Registrar Accreditation Board (RAB) 110, 112

registrars 109-117

registration *See certification.*

regulatory compliance *See compliance.*

steering committee 58, 66

structure of ISO 14000 35-39

structure of implementation process 67

surveillance audits 113, 117-118

151

sustainability *48, 74*

training *47, 67-69, 70, 82, 96-97, 100*

training internal auditors *98-100*

training plan, written *68*

training video, use of *68, 70-71*

Trus Joist *19-20, 48, 52, 80, 94-95*

U.S. Army, Ft. Lewis *See Ft. Lewis.*

volatile organic compounds (VOCs) *12*

waste *10, 12, 13, 17, 48, 57, 126-128*

wastewater *89, 124, 126*

About the Authors

John Kinsella has over 24 years of environmental management experience in North America, Europe, and Asia. He has provided environmental management system consulting and training to a wide range of organizations, including BC Hydro, British Petroleum, Hewlett Packard, Port of Portland, Weyerhaeuser Company, the U.S. Navy, and SEH-America.

A RAB-certified Lead EMS auditor, Kinsella is currently working with a team to integrate safety, security, and environment into an overall management system structure. He holds a B.A. from Trinity College Dublin and an M.Sc. from the University of London.

Annette Dennis McCully has been a science, business, and technical writer for 18 years, interviewing senior managers of corporations, governmental, and public organizations for case studies, procedures, and handbooks. Her clients include the Financial Consulting Solutions Group, Inc., the United Nations, Simmons Engineering and Scientific Communication, and Shaw Environmental, Inc.

A graduate of Goddard College in Vermont, McCully has a degree in management and is a RAB-certified EMS auditor. In 2001, she was awarded a fellowship at the University of Southern California's Annenberg School for Communication.

In 1998, McCully and Kinsella co-authored a self-study handbook, *Understanding and Implementing ISO 14001*, for the American Management Association. They co-authored the first edition of a *Handbook for Implementing an ISO 14001 Environmental Management System* in 1999. ∎

The authors can be reached by e-mail:

John Kinsella . . . . john.kinsella@shawgrp.com

Annette Dennis McCully . . . . amccully@aol.com